Biological conservation

Ian F. Spellerberg

Senior Lecturer in Biology and Director of Studies for Environmental Sciences, Southampton University

Steve Hardes

Head of Biology, Cricklade College, Andover

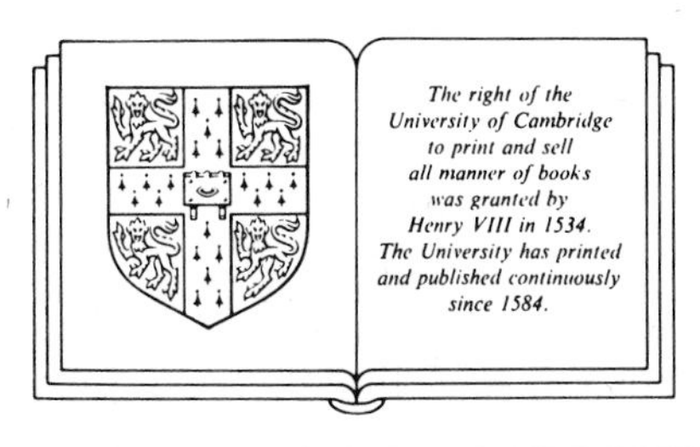

CAMBRIDGE UNIVERSITY PRESS
Cambridge
New York Port Chester Melbourne Sydney

Published by the Press Syndicate of the University of Cambridge
The Pitt Building, Trumpington Street, Cambridge CB2 1RP
40 West 20th Street, New York, NY 10011–4211, USA
10 Stamford Road, Oakleigh, Victoria 3166, Australia

First published 1992

Printed in Great Britain at the University Press, Cambridge

A catalogue record for this book is available from the British Library.

ISBN 0 521 39786 3 paperback

Cover photograph: Black rhino and calf © Stephen Krasemann/NHPA

Acknowledgements

Figures: 2.1, Meridian Design/Redwood; 3.1, copyright 1988 by the AAAS; 3.3, copyright 1982 by the AAAS; 3.9, 4.8, copyright New Scientist; 4.1 from H. Thorpe in J.G. Hawkes (1978) *Conservation and Agriculture*, Gerald Duckworth & Co; 4.5, by permission of Elsevier Science Publishing Company; 4.7, by kind permission of the Game Conservancy Trust.

Boxes: 1.1, with permission of the Beckman Foundation for the Environment; 4.9, Dr A.C. Jensen, Dr K.J. Collins & Professor A.P.M. Lockwood with support from National Power and Powergen; A1.1, map with permission of the Botanical Society of British Isles, early spider orchid by Jane Perry.

Tables: 3.1, courtesy of the Natural History Museum; 3.5, reprinted from *A Wealth of Wild Species: Storehouse of Human Welfare*, N. Myers (1983) by permission of Westview Press, Boulder, Colorado; 4.5, reprinted with permission from *Biodiversity*, © 1988 by the National Academy of Sciences, published by National Academy Press, Washington DC.

GO

Contents

Preface

The 1980s will be remembered for the rapidly growing concern for environmental issues, a concern which has slowly but surely spread throughout many countries. Membership of environmental organizations has increased dramatically, environmental issues are being discussed widely in the political arena and there have been attempts to cost the benefits of biological conservation.

What is perceived as the most important environmental issue depends on current events. For example, nuclear energy issues were much under discussion after the Chernobyl accident (1986) and oil spills were topical after the spill off the coast of Alaska (1989). Pollution, global warming, damage to the ozone layer, shortage of clean freshwater and energy conservation are perhaps seen as the most important environmental issues. All of these, especially global warming, are very important environmental issues, but perhaps of greater importance is the loss in species richness and genetic diversity. Species are becoming extinct faster than they can be described.

It could be argued that living organisms are our most important resource. They are not only a source of food and medicine but they also help to reduce levels of pollutants. Green plants (whether in the tropical forests, in the Arctic or in the sea) are the lungs of this Earth and help to maintain the carbon dioxide–oxygen balance. Plants, animals and their habitats also provide us with enjoyment and recreation. Biological conservation is not just about saving the large, appealing creatures from extinction. Biological conservation is based on science, including aspects of taxonomy, genetics, population biology, and ecology. It provides us with a basis for the management and conservation of living organisms, habitats and ecosystems, all of which affect the quality of our lives.

This book has been designed with practical conservation in mind. We have therefore included not only our personal view of conservation but also brief accounts of conservation in practice. The aims of this book are, therefore, to give an insight into the importance of biological conservation, to describe why conservation is important, to give examples of conservation and perhaps most importantly to generate enthusiasm, discussion and action.

This book could not have been possible without the generous and kind help of the following: Sue Cavey, Larry Edwards, Jane Evans, Peggy Sleigh, Andy Smith and Tom Stratford. We would especially like to thank Professor P.J. Kelly for his encouragement and guidance.

Postscript

Since writing this book there have been a number of important developments, indicative that biological conservation in practice is truly dynamic. For example, the sequel to the World Conservation Strategy (published in 1980) has been prepared by the IUCN and should be published in the autumn of 1991. In Britain, the Nature Conservancy Council and the Countryside Commission are being restructured as a result of the Environmental Protection Act, 1990. At present the organizations are as follows: Nature Conservancy Council for England (English Nature for short), Countryside Council for Wales, and Nature Conservancy Council for Scotland (which will combine with the Countryside Commission for Scotland in 1992 to form the Scottish Natural Heritage). The Joint Nature Conservation Committee coordinates national projects and represents British interests in Europe and abroad.

1

Biological conservation in context

1.1 What is biological conservation?

Biological conservation has an applied objective and has its origins in wildlife management and park management, which have long been supported by botanic gardens, zoological societies and conservation organizations. Today, biological conservation occurs in wilderness areas, in the countryside, in the oceans, in cities, in botanic gardens and zoos and in scientific laboratories.

There are different levels of conservation ranging from biosphere conservation to the conservation of single groups of plants and animals (fig 1.1). Biological conservation aims to maintain the diversity of living organisms, their habitats and the interrelationships between organisms and their environment. Biological conservation can be achieved using applied aspects of various sciences, including conservation biology (composed of taxonomy, ecology, genetics and other aspects of biology), biogeography and demography. That is, conservation of living organisms is the aim of biological conservation and that aim is achieved by the application of various sciences.

Biological conservation is not just about the conservation of plants and animals but is also directed at all aspects of life (biodiversity), including genetic material, populations, communities and ecosystems (fig 1.1). A **population** is a group of individuals of all the same species living in a defined area. A **community** is a group of populations of different species and an **ecosystem** consists of communities interacting with their environment. **Biodiversity** is a term which is used to refer to all of the diversity and variability of nature.

But what is meant by conservation, and is it the same as preservation? For some people, conservation means protection of wildlife from human

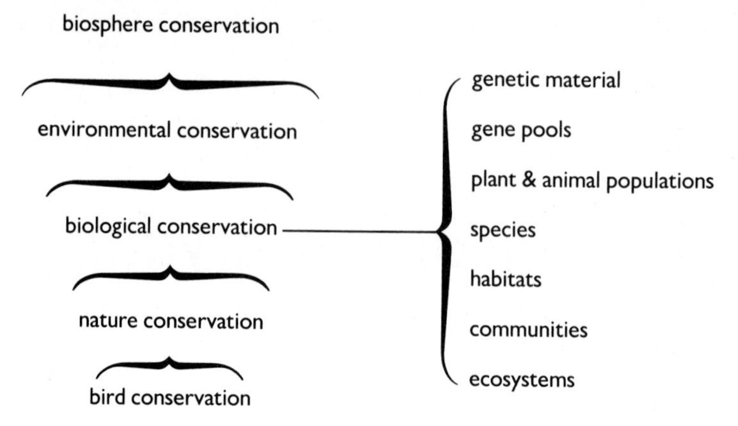

Fig 1.1 Levels of conservation in order of increasing breadth from single taxonomic groups (in this case birds) to biosphere conservation (including the atmosphere, ozone layer, water, minerals and energy, as well as living organisms). That is, biological conservation is part of environmental conservation.

exploitation whilst others consider that conservation should include an element of exploitation but on a sustainable basis. In other words there seem to be two alternatives: protect wildlife from any form of use, or conserve it in such a way that it will be of benefit to us and to future generations.

Preservation, in the strict sense, means keeping something without letting it change. Nature, however, is in a continuous state of change, through the seasons and by way of **ecological succession** from one type of community to another. For example, grassland may eventually become scrubland and then woodland, or bare sand dunes may become colonized with dune plants, to be replaced later by woodland. We cannot preserve habitats because they are always changing. The term conservation is therefore better than preservation, but whether we mean conservation as a way of protecting nature or as a way of using nature in a sustainable manner is open to discussion, as we hope you will find in the following sections of this book.

1.2 Biological conservation as a science

Why should biological conservation have a scientific basis? It is because from science we gain knowledge. The more we know about animals and plants, the more likely we are to be successful at conserving biodiversity. The same could be said about conserving habitats or ecosystems. The more we know about how they function, the better we will be able to manage or restore them and so conserve living organisms.

An example from the science of genetics provides an illustration. We know from genetical research that many rare animal and plant species are no longer viable; there is just not enough genetic variation present in the remnant populations, and in some cases they are too inbred to enable them to survive in changing conditions. The populations of many large mammals, such as species of rhinoceros, cheetah and populations of many tropical plants are examples. The variation amongst individuals of these species has reached such a low level that they would become extinct if there were significant changes in their environment. Larger populations tend to have more individuals with a greater range of genetic variability so that at least some individuals will survive in a changing environment. Many rare plants and animals are now kept in botanic gardens or zoos where attempts are made to increase the populations with the aim of being able to return individuals to the wild. This approach to conservation is termed 'ex situ' conservation as opposed to conservation of plant and animals in their natural environment ('in situ' conservation). The conservation of all species of rhinoceros will therefore depend on their protection from exploitation, conservation of their habitat (in situ conservation) and breeding programmes in zoos (ex situ conservation).

1.3 Other approaches to conservation

Not all biological conservation has a traditional scientific basis. Some conservation is achieved because of the perceived dependence of humans (for their survival) on living organisms. Some religions include elements of conservation and many cultures throughout the world have a very close relationship with the living environment. Populations of many indigenous peoples live in 'harmony' with nature; for example two celebrated examples of people living with nature in a most remarkable and successful way are the Waorani of Ecuador (see fig 3.8) and the Aborigines of Australia.

Another approach to conservation was demonstrated in 1973, by the Norwegian philosopher Arne Naess who coined the term 'deep ecology' in an attempt to go beyond ecology as a science to a deeper level of self-awareness and 'Earth Wisdom'. The essence of deep ecology is to keep asking more searching questions about human life and society and nature. The concept has since been developed by several people, especially Devall & Sessions (1985). The underlying principles include 'The well-being and flourishing of non-human life on Earth have value in themselves, independent of the usefulness of the non-human world for human purposes' and 'Richness and diversity of life-forms contribute to the realization of these values and are also values in themselves'. There are today those who support deep ecology but also those who are gravely suspicious of what deep ecology stands for, and there is also much controversy between supporters of deep ecology and similar concepts.

In 1979 Lovelock published his book called *Gaia: a new look at life on earth* and that book has influenced many people and the way they view life on Earth. Gaia was the Greek goddess of the Earth. The Gaia hypothesis postulates that the physical and chemical conditions of the surface of the Earth, of the atmosphere and of the oceans, has been and is actively made fit and comfortable by the presence of life itself; that is the biosphere is a self-regulating entity with the capacity to keep our planet healthy by controlling the chemical and physical environment. This is in contrast to the more conventional idea that life has evolved and adapted to the Earth's conditions. Thus by conserving living things, Lovelock would argue, you maintain the totality of the Earth's existence.

1.4 The value and importance of conservation

What is so important about biological conservation? To answer this question we could consider two levels of importance: global importance and importance to the individual. Biological conservation is taking place throughout the world (see the examples in box 1.1) but we need look no further than the World Conservation Strategy, published in 1980, for statements of value and importance (box 2.1).

1 The maintenance of essential ecological processes and life support systems;
2 the conservation of genetic diversity and wild species;
3 the sustainable utilization of species and ecosystems – to use all our natural resources carefully giving due consideration to the needs of future generations.

But is biological conservation important to you, the individual, and do you have a view on the value of conservation? To answer these questions, we surveyed some students and asked the following questions.

A What is biological conservation?
B If you believe biological conservation is important, then why is it important?
C Can you suggest how you might contribute to biological conservation?

Before reading any further, perhaps you might like to give an answer to each question yourself. How do your answers compare with those in table 1.1? Although some answers to the first question incorrectly equated biological conservation with environmental conservation, we feel that the answers indicate a deep insight to and understanding of many aspects of biological conservation. There were some surprising answers about the importance of biological conservation but the majority felt that biological conservation was important in that it helped to prevent extinction. An interesting follow-up question would be 'What is important about preventing extinction?' In later parts of this book we will come back to this important issue.

It was interesting to see that biological conservation was seen as being important, not only from a biological or scientific point of view but also from an enjoyment or amenity perspective. In addition to the moral

AROUND THE WORLD

At least four white tail sea eagle chicks have been successfully reared from captive bred birds from Germany. These eagles, which disappeared from Czechoslovakia in the 1850s, have been released in the natural reserve of Velky Tisy . . .

Some success is reported in the reintroduction to the wild of the large blue butterfly (Maculinea arion) in the UK following its extinction there in 1979. About 75 adults were bred in 1987, laying in total more than 2000 eggs. Several new colonies have now been established and research into ecological requirements has been extended to include four other species of large blue . . .

Drainage of wetlands and extensive use of pesticides are two reasons for the imminent extinction of the wild hermit ibis (Geronica eremita) in Europe. Once a common sight in central Europe, just three birds returned from migration in 1989 to eastern Turkey. Two of these were killed in a storm and it is thought that the one remaining is the last wild member of the species . . .

Scientists at Tel Aviv University have reported what is believed to be the first captive hatching of the Negev lappet-faced vulture. There is only one known wild pair remaining in the Negev Desert where loss of food supply and excessive hunting rendered the species almost extinct . . .

Following two successful years of captive breeding of the black-footed ferret at Sybille, Wyoming, USA, two additional populations are being established. Ten captive pairs have each been placed with the National Zoological Park's Conservation and Research Centre in Front Royal, Virginia, and with the Henry Doorly Zoo in Omaha, Nebraska. The objective is to make available a total of 250 breeding pairs so that a reintroduction programme to re-establish wild colonies can commence in 1991. Prairie dogs are the ferrets' primary source of food. Population counts of these animals are being undertaken to identify appropriate sites for release of the ferrets . . .

Protection programmes for the red kite in the UK have resulted in an increase in these birds in Wales. Up to about 1890, the red kite was fairly often seen in the country but human persecution caused its virtual disappearance at the end of the last century. The few remaining in Wales received protection. Now about 50 pairs exist which, with others from Sweden, form the nucleus of hope for their reintroduction to parts of England and Scotland.

The Manchurian tiger may have become extinct in the wild in China. None has been sighted in aerial surveys and there is fear that the only remaining population in China may be the 20 captive in zoos. The tiger's demise is undoubtedly due to human destruction of forest habitats and excessive poaching . . .

The European Community has permanently banned the importation of baby sealskins, replacing a six-year restriction which expired in the Autumn . . .

The leatherback turtle continues to decline (only 100 came ashore in Terengganu State, Malaysia, to nest in 1988 compared with over 1500 in 1956). As a useful gesture the State Government has amended the Turtles Enactment 1987 so that anyone possessing an egg of the leatherback could be fined $385, imprisoned for six months, or both . . .

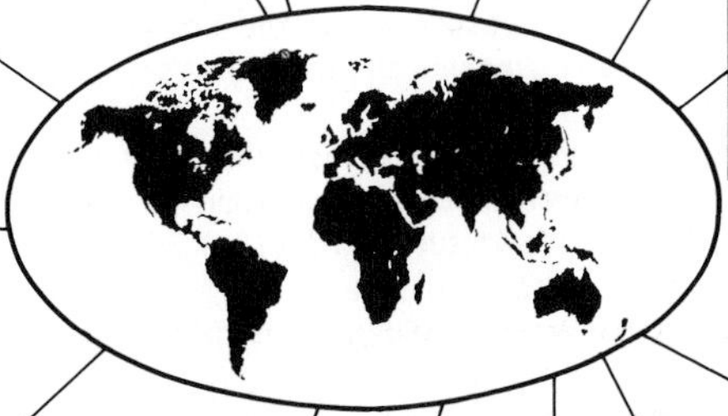

Only 34 Puerto Rican parrots (Amazona vittata) remain in the wild, according to a count carried out recently in the Carribean National Forest, Puerto Rico. Two pairs in a captive rearing centre there hatched three eggs last year . . .

A campaign is being mounted in New Zealand by the Royal Forest and Bird Protection Society to persuade the Government to ban the export of native wood chip, part of a flourishing trade with Japan. The result of the trade is substantial destruction of beech forests on South Island with each wood chip load leaving Nelson by ship accounting for about 350 ha of beech forest — a habitat for at least 2500 native birds as well as countless numbers of other species . . .

A report from the Emperor Valley Zoo in Trinidad highlights the first captive breeding of the South American giant river turtle (Podocnemis expansa). The announcement is particularly significant in that the breeding turtles are survivors of a group captured 64 years ago which had never before reproduced. Zoo officials consider that the success is due to manipulation of water levels in the turtles' pool and the provision of an area of deep, clean sand at the pool's edge . . .

The forests of Rwanda, a major habitat of the threatened mountain gorilla, contains over 500 species of birds. The forests attracted more than 8000 tourists in 1989 . . .

A rubbish dump near Hamilton, Australia, has been the site of the only remaining colony of eastern-barred bandicoots (Perameles gunii). A few hundred animals were reported to survive there. A Bicentennial Grant has resulted in the establishment of a new colony at a somewhat safer site at Gellibrand Hill Park near Melbourne Airport . . .

The market for sharks' fins is rapidly expanding, especially in Hong Kong, Singapore and Tokyo, where there is a large restaurant demand. High prices paid for the fins encourage fishermen in small vessels to discard the remainder of the shark. The USA Mid-Atlantic Fishery Management Council has called for restrictions on fishing, anticipating depletion of these creatures which are particularly slow in growing and reaching maturity . . .

Australia has proposed a regional ban on drift net fishing in the South Pacific. This method, though intended for catching tuna and salmon, indiscriminately nets and kills dolphins, whales, turtles and seals. Between 20,000 and 40,000 tonnes of tuna — more than twice the maximum recommended catch — were caught in 1988, mainly by a fleet of 160 boats operating in the South Pacific. 130 of these are from Taiwan and 30 from Japan, which has now banned use of these nets within 160km of its own coast . . .

Box 1.1. Biological conservation around the world. From *Biosphere* (winter 1990), the publication of the Beckman Foundation for the Environment.

Table 1.1 *A compilation of the main kinds of answers from young people (13–19) in response to three questions about biological conservation.*

A	**What is biological conservation?**
1	Preserving (protecting) our environment or natural areas or natural habitats. (26%)
2	Preserving animals and plants. (14%)
3	Preservation, protecting, saving threatened or endangered species. (10%)
4	Protection of fauna and flora – of the world. (8%)
5	Protecting habitats and endangered species. (6%)
6	Preventing extinction of plants and animals. (6%)
7	Preventing damage or being aware of damage to natural areas. (6%)
8	Maintenance, management of natural resources, ecosystems, natural areas. (5%)
9	Keeping an ecological balance – balance of nature. (3%)
10	Conservation of animal and plant species and nature. (3%)
11	Maintenance, preservation of diversity of threatened species. (3%)
12	Continuation of the environment, nature – cohabitation. (2%)
13	Protection of the Earth, Earth's ecosystems. (2%)
14	Preservation/conservation of certain species perceived to be of value to society. (2%)
15	No answer. (2%)
16	Using 'environmentally friendly' products. (1%)
B	**If you believe biological conservation is important then why is it important?**
1	It's (morally) wrong to make/let species become extinct. (24%)
2	It provides pleasure, beauty, amenity, an escape or it's important psychologically and aesthetically. (16%)
3	It's just important – plant and animal species are important. (11%)
4	Helps maintain a healthy environment, helps sustain life. (11%)
5	To let future generations enjoy nature. (11%)
6	Helps maintain the global ecosystem. (7%)
7	Without conservation we would lose organisms important for horticulture, agriculture, medicine. (5%)
8	Prevents industry, modern life destroying nature. (5%)
9	Maintains genetic and species diversity. (4%)
10	Not enough known about nature, natural beauty. (1%)
11	It's the only world we've got. (1%)
12	Respect for Gaia. (1%)
13	Keeps old traditions alive. (1%)
14	Don't know. (1%)
C	**Can you suggest how you might contribute to biological conservation?**
1	No answer or said 'don't know'. (39%)
2	Support or join an environmental/conservation organization. (24%)
3	Avoid using harmful chemicals, choose environmentally friendly consumer goods. (8%)
4	Don't destroy habitats and flowers. (5%)
5	Recycle. (5%)
6	Help to protect green areas and offer practical help. (5%)
7	Write letters, get involved in the 'politics' of conservation. (3%)
8	Give money to conservation organizations, projects. (2%)
9	Observe protection/conservation codes and rules. (2%)
10	Study and learn about conservation. (2%)
11	Bring down imperialists, change the politics. (1%)
12	Identify areas in need of conservation. (1%)
13	Prevent intensive agriculture, forestry etc. (1%)
14	Don't pollute. (1%)
15	Don't buy animal products. (1%)

Table 1.2 *Suggested 'values' and functions of biodiversity.*

A	**Ethical and moral values**
1	Intrinsic value of nature.
2	Natural world has value as a human heritage.
B	**Enjoyment and aesthetic values**
1	Leisure activities ranging from bird watching to walking.
2	Sporting activities ranging from orienteering to diving.
3	Aesthetic value by way of seeing, hearing or touching wildlife.
4	Enjoyment of nature depicted in art.
C	**Use as a resource for food, materials, research inspiration and education (utilitarian)**
1	As a genetic resource for some of the following.
2	As a source of food.
3	Source of working animals.
4	As a source of pharmaceutical products.
5	As a source of materials for buildings.
6	As a source of materials for making goods.
7	As a source of fuel for energy.
8	As a source of organisms for biological control.
9	For scientific research.
10	Educational value.
11	Inspiration for technological development.
D	**Maintenance of the environment (ecosystems and climates)**
1	Role in maintaining CO_2/O_2 balance.
2	Role in maintaining water cycles and maintaining water catchments.
3	Role in absorbing waste materials.
4	Role in determining the nature of world climates, regional climates and microclimates.
5	Indicators of environmental change.
6	Protection from harmful weather conditions: wind breaks, flood barriers.

arguments we could identify three main values of biological conservation; for enjoyment, as a material and scientific resource (utilitarian) and for maintaining ecosystems and affecting climates (table 1.2). The 11 utilitarian functions of nature range from the use of genetic material (such as for improving crop and grazing plants) to ideas for technology. Nature has given us many ideas for the advancement of technology, for example studies of how flies use their wings and halteres gave important data for the design and subsequent application of gyroscopes in various modes of transport.

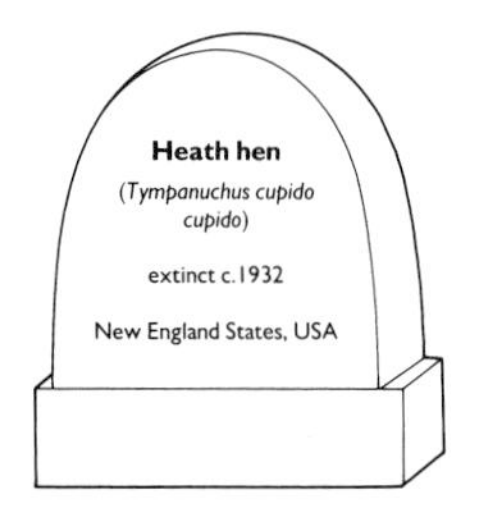

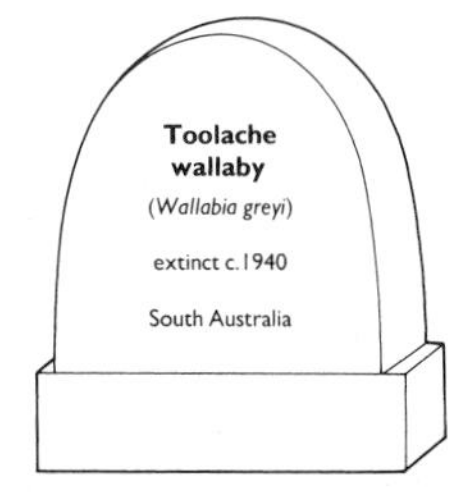

2

The growth and development of conservation

Table 2.1 is a list of some events which have made environmental and biological conservation more and more prominent over the last 100 years. The establishment of conservation organizations, the implementation of wildlife law, international meetings, seminars and treaties have all influenced the way in which conservation has grown and developed. Conservation organizations have played a particularly important role in shaping the direction of biological conservation. Many governments around the world have established wildlife and conservation organizations. In the USA, for example, The Fish and Wildlife Service is responsible, amongst other things, for the National Wildlife Refuge System which is the world's largest and most diverse collection of protected areas for conservation. The Fish and Wildlife Service undertakes a wide variety of research on conservation, some by way of the Patuxent Wildlife Research Center, based at Laurel in Maryland but with research stations throughout the USA. In Britain, the Nature Conservancy Council is the organization responsible for the designation and management of National Nature reserves and other kinds of protected areas.

There are also thousands of voluntary, non-governmental conservation and environmental organizations located in many countries. For example there is the Nature Conservancy in the USA and the Royal Society for Protection of Birds in Britain (membership of 3/4 million in 1990), both of which make very important and effective contributions to conservation. Two organizations in particular have dominated the international conservation scene and they are the International Union for the Conservation of Nature (IUCN) and the World Wide Fund for Nature (WWF). In this chapter we take a brief look at these two organizations as well as some of the literature and wildlife law which has contributed to the growth and development of biological conservation.

Table 2.1 *The shaping of environmental conservation and biological conservation – important events. (A list of some organizations is given in appendix 2.)*

1884	The American Ornithologist's Union forms a committee for 'the protection of North American Birds and their eggs . . .'
1885	The US Department of Agriculture established a division of economic ornithology and mammalogy which later became the biological survey and then the US Fish and Wildlife Service.
1889	The Royal Society for the Protection of Birds (RSPB) is established in Britain, by a group of society ladies.
1892	The Sierra Club is founded in the USA.
1902	The New York Botanical Garden organizes the Wild Flower Preservation Society of America.
1903	President Theodore Roosevelt designates a 1.2 ha sanctuary for pelicans and herons. The Fauna and Flora Preservation Society is established in Britain.
1912	The Royal Society for Nature Conservation is established in Britain, on the initiative of Lord Rothschild.
1913	The British Ecological Society is formed.
1918	The Save-the-Redwoods League is formed in California.
1922	The International Council for Bird Preservation is founded.
1948	United Nations Charter published. International Union for the Protection of Nature (IUPN) established.
1957	The IUPN becomes the International Union for the Conservation of Nature and Natural Resources (IUCN)
1958	The first UN Conference on the Law of the Sea, approves draft conventions on environmental protection.
1959	Antarctic Treaty established. The UN Economic and Social Council adopts a resolution to publish a register of the world's national parks and similar protected areas.
1961	World Wild Life Fund established (World Wide Fund for Nature, WWF), largely on the initiative of Sir Peter Scott.
1963	Moscow Treaty: banning nuclear weapon tests in the atmosphere, in outer space and underwater.
1967	Torrey Canyon oil spill off Wales.
1969	Friends of the Earth is founded in America.
1970	April 21 was Earth Day in the USA when 20 million people participated in peaceful demonstrations; Earth Day was probably the launch of the environmental movement in that country.
1971	Green peace is launched. Friends of the Earth established in Britain.
1972	United Nations Conference on the Human Environment. United Nations Environment Programme established.
1973	World oil shortage.
1977	United Nations Conference on Desertification.
1978	Amoco Cadiz oil spill off France.
1979	Three Mile Island nuclear incident.

Table 2.1 (*cont.*)

1979	Greenhouse effect: a world climate conference in Geneva concludes that there is a greenhouse effect as a result of accumulation of carbon dioxide.
1980	Brandt Commission: north–south, a programme for survival.
1982	Second Brandt Commission. UN Nairobi Conference (follow-up to Stockholm). German Green Party established with national parliamentary seats.
1984	WWF/IUCN Plant Conservation Programme launched. Bhopal chemical disaster in India.
1985	International Conference on the assessment of carbon dioxide and other greenhouse gases in climatic variation. A meeting of 200 scientists at the Second Conference on Conservation Biology at the University of Michigan agree to launch a new Society devoted to Conservation Biology.
1986	Chernobyl nuclear accident. Pollution of the Rhine reaches dramatic levels. Greenpeace ship Rainbow Warrier sunk by a bomb in Auckland.
1987	World Commission on Environment and Development established. Montreal Ozone Treaty. The Society for Conservation Biology holds its first meeting in Bozeman, Montana, USA.
1988	Hurricane Joan destroys 3600 square miles of virgin rainforest in Nicaragua, Central America.
1989	The Exxon Valdez oil spill in Prince William Sound, Alaska. Ozone layer conference. The 'Green Summit': meeting of seven major industrial countries in Paris, with a final communique entitled 'Urgent need to safeguard the environment'.
1990–1	A global survival strategy is advocated. The UN Secretary General (Javier Perez de Cuellar) suggested that the UN produce a global environment strategy for the next UN Environmental Conference.
1991	The Gulf war. The largest oil spill to date occurred after the blowing up of Kuwaiti oil fields.

2.1 The International Union for the Conservation of Nature and the World Wide Fund for Nature

The establishment of the International Union for the Protection of Nature (IUPN) in 1948 and the World Wide Fund for Nature 13 years later were important milestones in conservation history. In 1957 the IUPN was reorganized and renamed the International Union for the Conservation of Nature and Natural Resources. There are very strong links between the IUCN and the WWF, especially as the WWF has been a major source of finance for the IUCN.

Established in 1961, WWF is now represented in over 24 countries and raises money for conservation projects in all parts of the world (fig 2.1). By 1989, WWF had raised nearly £82 million for over 5000 projects in 130 countries. As well as fund raising for conservation of both species and habitats, WWF contributes in a major way to conservation policies in many countries and also publishes reports and statements about various conservation issues.

The IUCN has its headquarters in Gland, Switzerland and has offices throughout the world (such as in Pakistan, Costa Rica, Zimbabwe, Senegal, Kenya, Germany, USA and the UK). There is a membership of nearly 640, made up of both non-governmental organizations (NGOs), such as the Sierra Club of the USA and the British Ecological Society, and member countries. The IUCN promotes many activities, including cooperation between conservation organizations, scientific research, conservation education, international agreements, conservation legislation and generally takes any other form of action to promote the conservation of the world's wildlife and natural resources. Much of the work of the IUCN is carried out through scientific commissions and centres, such as the World Conservation Monitoring Centre which is based at Cambridge and at the Royal Botanic Gardens, Kew. There are six scientific commissions which have been responsible for species protection, protected areas, conservation education and training, wildlife law, ecology and planning. The IUCN also undertakes 'theme'-based conservation activities resulting in major contributions to conservation of tropical forest, wetland and marine ecosystems.

Within the past few years the IUCN has worked with governments to secure improved effectiveness of protected areas and to achieve a better understanding of the environmental implications arising out of economic development in Third World countries. These activities have taken place in many countries, including Botswana, Costa Rica, China, Oman, Pakistan and Zambia. The IUCN has collaborated with various agencies to protect areas in Indonesia (with the World Bank), to conserve the Giant Panda in China (with the WWF), and to promote conservation of forests and water supplies in Tanzania (with the Norwegian Agency for International Development – NORAD). Authoritative publications, reviews and policy documents are published by the IUCN and these include Red Data Books (see p. 15), directories and guides for management of protected areas. An important contribution made by IUCN to the conservation of the world's resources has come by way of helping to establish national treaties and legislation in the form of conventions (see p. 17).

2.2 Biological conservation publications

In the 1950s and 1960s agricultural land, forests, gardens, lawns, roadsides and urban gardens in North America were being regularly sprayed with an assortment of chemicals. The implications of this intensive use of insecticides and herbicides were described in a provocative book called *Silent Spring*, written by Rachel Carson. She contended that the widespread use of agricultural chemicals (including DDT) seemed to

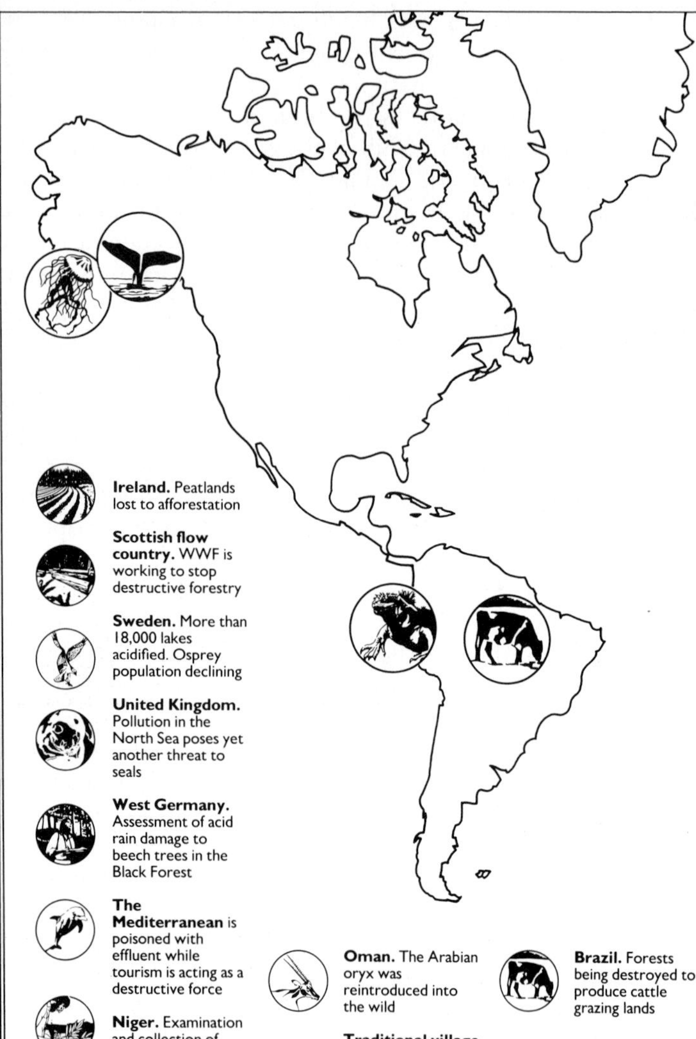

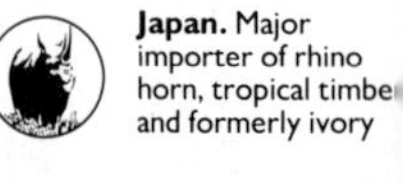
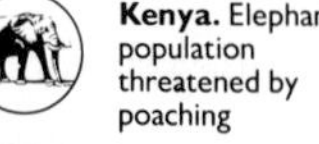

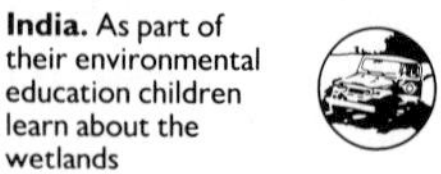

Fig 2.1 The international work of the World Wide Fund for Nature – biological conservation is not just saving species! (from *WWF Review, news and analysis of WWF's operations in 1988/89*).

- Helping people in unstable environments help themselves
- Saving threatened species

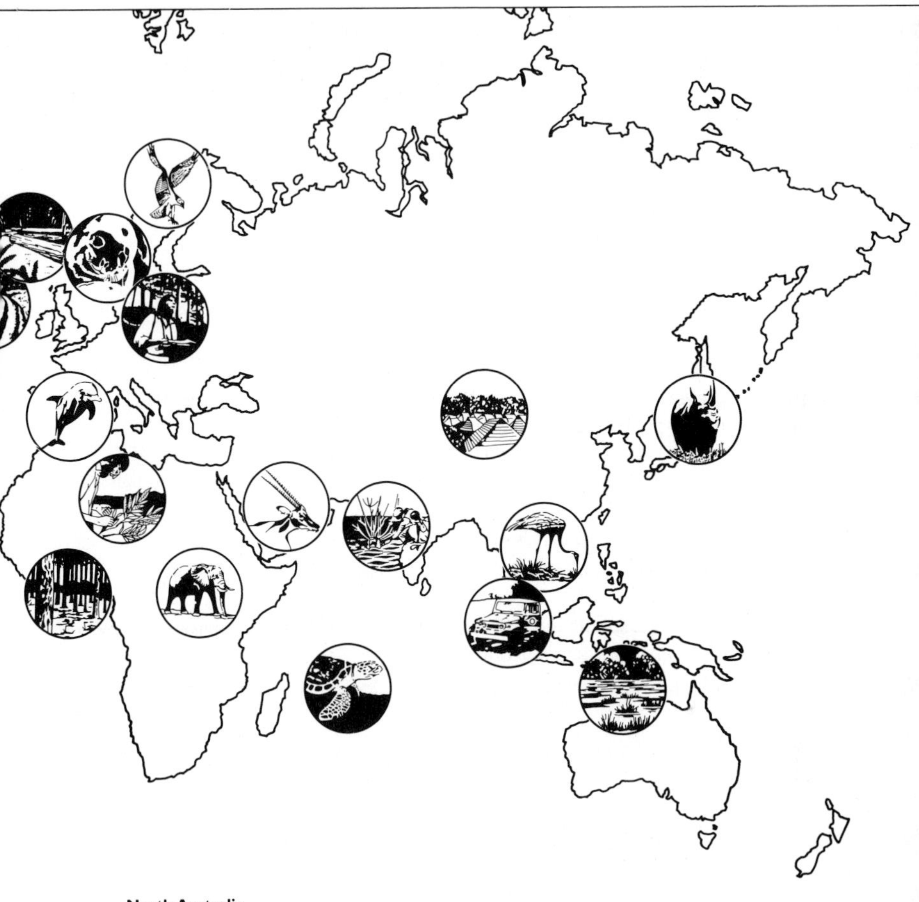

North Australia. Billabong at risk during the dry season. WWF has several important projects in Australia

Alaska. The oil spill continues to threaten marine life

Iguana on Santa Cruz, one of the Galapagos Islands – a vital conservation project

Vietnam wetlands under threat

Tail fluke of humpback whale in Alaska. WWF has been campaigning worldwide to stop the killing of whales.

Studying the medicinal plants in one of WWF's major projects, Korup, Cameroon will enable the local people to harness the rainforest's natural chemistry

GLOBAL ALERT

WWF is working on every continent to stop environmental destruction, as these examples show

Table 2.2 *Some 'milestone' conservation publications (see bibliography).*

1864	*Man & Nature; Or Physical Geography as Modified by Human Action* Marsh, G.P. (New York, Scribners. London, Sampson & Low). An early statement about concern for the future of wildlife.
1945	*Our Heritage of Wild Nature: a Plea for Organized Nature Conservation* Tansley, A.G. (Cambridge, Cambridge University Press). Influenced decision makers in Britain.
1948	*Our Plundered Planet* Osborn, F. (Boston, Little Brown). A perceptive book by an investment banker about limits of environmental resources.
1956	*Man's Role in Changing the Face of the Earth* Thomas, W.L. (ed.) (Chicago, The University of Chicago Press). Several authors draw attention to dramatic reduction and fragmentation of natural areas.
1962	*Silent Spring* Carson, R. (Boston, Mass., Houghton-Mifflin). Recognition of the damage caused by very wide and extensive use of pesticides.
1966	*First Red Data Book* (Gland, IUCN). Synoptic information on endangered species and statement of the degree of threat.
1968	The scientific journal *Biological Conservation* is launched.
1972	*A Blueprint for Survival* Goldsmith, E. *et al.* (In *The Ecologist*, **2**, no. 1, January 1972). Global environmental problems. *The Limits To Growth: A Report for the Club of Rome's Project on the Predicament of Mankind.* Meadows et *al.* (New York, Universe Books). Attention drawn to human population growth and diminishing resources.
1974	The scientific journal *Environmental Conservation* is launched.
1980	*World Conservation Strategy* (IUCN). Living resource conservation for sustainable development. The *Global 2000* report is submitted to President Carter. A document about serious lack of resources and environmental problems.
1982	*World Charter for Nature* (United Nations). Proclamation on the conservation of nature.
1984	*The Resourceful Earth. A Response to Global 2000* is published. Simon & Kahn (New York, Blackwell). An optimistic view about the environment, populations and resources.
1985	*Deep Ecology: Living as if Nature Mattered.* Devall & Sessions give a new and inspiring meaning to ecology and nature.
1987	*Our Common Future* (World Commission on Environment and Development). Statement of environmental concerns and common challenges, including human populations, energy, pollution, species, ecosystems and sustainable development.
1988	*Wildlands: their Protection and Management in Economic Development* (the World Bank). World economics enters the conservation arena at last.

threaten all wildlife to the extent that spring might not be heralded by bird song and wildflowers (thus the provocative title *Silent Spring*).

The publication of Rachel Carson's book could be said to have initiated current widespread concern about the use of chemicals in the environment and was thus one important 'milestone' publication (table 2.2). Nine years after *Silent Spring*, a journal called the *Ecologist* published *A Blueprint for Survival*. The *Blueprint* was a manifesto for social change to deal with the environmental issues as perceived in the early 1970s and was supported by many distinguished scientists. Like *Silent Spring*, the *Blueprint* initiated widespread discussion, especially in the scientific literature but it also had its critics. Some of those critics described the *Blueprint* as hysteria made up of half-baked anxieties. Looking back, the *Blueprint* does not seem to have been taken seriously, yet it may have had a major influence in the development of the IUCN World Conservation Strategy (box 2.1).

The World Conservation Strategy was produced by the IUCN in 1980 with the financial support of the WWF and the FAO (Food and Agricultural Organization of the United Nations) and was subtitled *Living resource conservation for sustainable development*. This bold publication attempted to address and focus the world's attention on conservation issues. Many countries have now responded to the World Conservation Strategy by producing national strategies. If nothing else, it convinced many governments of the importance of biological conservation.

Many reports and publications are produced by the IUCN, but perhaps the most famous have been the World Conservation Strategy and the International Red Data Books. The Red Data Books give information on the threatened plant and animal species of the world and are produced with the voluntary help of many thousands of scientists and lay people. That information is essential for the design of conservation programmes.

In 1982 the United Nations published the World Charter for Nature and one year later established a World Commission on the Environment and Development to consider the full consequences of species loss, desertification, global warming and other environmental and population problems. That Commission chaired by Mrs Brundtland, then Prime Minister of Norway, took 900 days to collect, assemble, synthesize and publish their report, *Our Common Future*. It is said by some to have been the most important document on the state of the world's resources to be published in the 1980s. During those 900 days there were, ironically, many environmental disasters and tragedies: such as the drought-triggered environmental crises in Africa putting 35 million at risk, the leak from a pesticides factory in Bhopal, India, which killed more than 2000 people and injured 200 000 more, the Chernobyl nuclear reactor accident, a major pollution incident in the Rhine, an estimated 60 million people died of diseases related to poor drinking water and malnutrition – most were children.

2.3 Wildlife law

Many countries have their own laws which help to protect areas for conservation and various species from harm. However, biological conservation can not be confined by political barriers and, therefore, international law has been essential for conservation efforts. Wildlife conventions have been initiated by many organizations, but noteably the IUCN and UNESCO (United Nations Educational, Scientific and Cultural Organization). Conservation issues are brought to the attention of such organizations by a variety of interested groups in different countries and, when

The World Conservation Strategy is intended to stimulate a more focused approach to the management of living resources and to provide policy guidance on how this can be carried out.

The aim of the World Conservation Strategy is to achieve the three main objectives of living resource conservation:

a. to maintain essential ecological processes and life-support systems (such as soil regeneration and protection, the recycling of nutrients, and the cleansing of waters), on which human survival and development depend;
b. to preserve genetic diversity (the range of genetic material found in the world's organisms), on which depend the functioning of many of the above processes and life-support systems, the breeding programmes necessary for the protection and improvement of cultivated plants, domesticated animals and microorganisms, as well as much scientific and medical advance, technical innovation, and the security of the many industries that use living resources;
c. to ensure the sustainable utilization of species and ecosystems (notably fish and other wildlife, forests and grazing lands), which support millions of rural communities as well as major industries.

These objectives must be achieved as a matter of urgency because:

a. the planet's capacity to support people is being irreversibly reduced in both developing and developed countries:
b. hundreds of millions of rural people in developing countries, including 500 million malnourished and 800 million destitute, are compelled to destroy the resources necessary to free them from starvation and poverty;
c. the energy, financial and other costs of providing goods and services are growing;
d. the resource base of major industries is shrinking.

Box 2.1 The World Conservation Strategy.

opinions are strong and a cause appears valid, an international conference is called for. This is then followed by countries becoming signatories and later ratifying the convention. The convention becomes law when an agreed number of countries ratify or give formal approval to the convention.

Table 2.3 *Examples of national and international Wildlife Conventions (based on Lyster 1985).*

1 **The International Convention for the Regulation of Whaling.**
The 'Whaling Convention' aims to protect whales from overexploitation, but at the same time achieve optimum levels of whale stocks. Thus conservation and development of the whaling industry are intertwined.

2 **The International Convention for the Protection of Birds.**
Known as the '1950 Bird Convention', this now has little 'practical impact on the policies of its party governments'.

3 **Conventions protecting the vicuna (*Vicugna vicugna*).**
There are three conventions protecting this species which is reputed to have the finest wool in the world.

4 **The Convention on the Conservation of European Wildlife and Natural Habitats.**
The 'Berne Convention' came into force in 1982 and aims to conserve wild fauna and flora in their natural habitats. By 1986 17 states out of 20 signatories had ratified this Convention.

5 **The African Convention on the Conservation of Nature and Natural Resources.**
This emphasizes the need to establish conservation areas and has the objective of ensuring conservation, utilization and development of natural resources.

6 **The Convention on the Conservation of Antarctic Marine Living Resources.**
Originating in the 1959 Antarctic Treaty, this Convention (CCAMLR) came into force in 1981 and has established a Commission, a Secretariat and a Scientific Committee and deals with a wide variety of issues relating to the entire area south of 60°.

7 **The Convention of Wetlands of International Importance.**
Around 300 wetland sites are in the 'Ramsar' list of Wetlands of International Importance.

8 **The Convention on International Trade in Endangered Species of Wild Fauna and Flora.**
The 'CITES' convention (ratified by 91 countries) attempts to control the multi-million dollar business in wildlife and wildlife products such as skins, horns, rare orchids and rare parrots.

9 **The Convention on Conservation of Migratory Species of Wild Animals.**
Many species of migratory birds and other animals are protected while in their breeding location but suffer from exploitation when migrating or in their winter habitat. The 'Bonn Convention' aims to provide strict protection for such species ranging from Dorcas Gazelles to Siberian Cranes and some insects.

Two examples of conventions are the Berne Convention and the Ramsar Convention (table 2.3). The aim of the Berne Convention is to conserve European wild fauna and flora and their habitats with particular emphasis on endangered and vulnerable species. Appendices in the Convention list the protected species, but these species lists are by no means comprehensive. Not all of Europe's vulnerable and endangered plant species are listed and therefore some biological conservation organizations feel that this Convention is limited in its scope and effectiveness. The Ramsar Convention addresses problems of the world's wetlands on a regional basis; wetlands are some of the most sensitive, yet most productive, of all ecosystems. For the purpose of this Convention, the key wetland sites are identified for reason of their international importance as habitats for wildfowl and wading birds.

Some countries such as the USA have been strengthening their conservation laws in such a way as to protect species from widespread exploitation. In 1988, the then President Reagan signed a bill to strengthen the US Endangered Species Act which, amongst other things, will help protect African elephant populations which have declined by about 50% in the ten years since 1979. Their decline has been caused by habitat destruction and exploitation for ivory. A special section of the bill enables the establishment of limits on imports of raw and worked ivory into the USA to help prevent poaching.

In the UK there has been relatively slow progress in establishing laws which contribute towards the conservation of plants, animals and their habitats. Some groups of animals such as birds, deer and badgers have received special protection and acts, such as the Countryside Act 1968, have provided a means for the establishment and protection of Sites of Special Scientific Interest (SSSI). It was not until 1975 that the UK had an act which gave protection to several groups of animals and plants. The oddly named Conservation of Wild Creatures and Wild Plants Act of 1975 had a curious list of animals which were given protection, curious in that there seemed to be no agreed criteria for their selection. This Act has since been replaced by the Wildlife and Countryside Act (1981) which, amongst other things, affords protection to plants, birds and a wide range of other animals. Like many other examples of wildlife law the 1981 Act does not necessarily protect all species which are endangered or threatened. This is because it is not easy to decide which criteria should be used for the selection of species to be protected. Although ecological criteria such as distribution and decline in population size can be measured accurately, other criteria such as attractiveness of the species are more difficult to apply. Nevertheless, it is possible to quantify features such as attractiveness or vulnerability to collection, be it in a simple manner (see section A1.4).

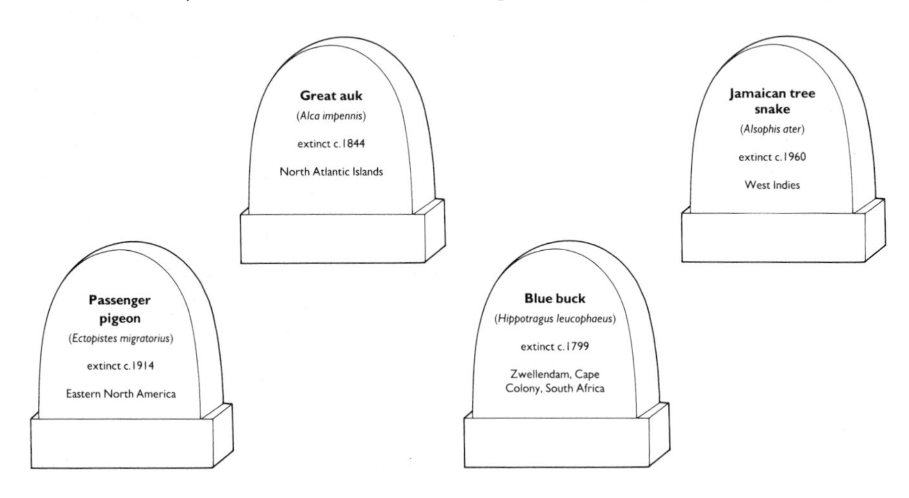

3

Why conserve nature?

For many of us the need to conserve wildlife is something that we just accept as right. In any scientific discipline, though, it is necessary to be objective. To this end we have considered the question 'Why conserve nature?' in two ways. Firstly by examining the current losses in biological diversity and the impact of humans in relation to these losses, and secondly by attempting to assess the value of diversity.

3.1 Losses in biological diversity

Biological diversity

At the last count there were approximately 1.7 million named living species (table 3.1). Various estimates place the actual number between 5 and in excess of 30 million (box 3.1). It is unlikely that the true figure will ever be known, however, because human activity is causing the extinction of species before they have been recorded.

The species is the basic taxonomic unit, but the gene pool which unites the members of species is often large and may be continually changing. Consequently within a species there exists a considerable variety of forms. These may be sufficiently different to warrant the status of subspecies or race (fig 3.2). Such diversity is a form of organic insurance against a changing environment. If there is a dramatic change, a few individuals at least are equipped to survive, thereby ensuring the continuance of the species.

Extinctions

The fossil record reveals a continually changing pattern of biological diversity. The number of species alive today is thought to represent a

Table 3.1 *Approximate number of named living species (from P. Whitehead & C. Keates,* British Museum (Natural History), *(Scala Wilson, 1981)).*

Animals	
Sponges	10 000
Corals, jellyfish etc.	10 000
Flatworms	25 000
Roundworms	30 000
Molluscs	110 000
Earthworms etc.	15 000
Spiders, scorpions, mites etc.	130 000
Crustaceans	30 000
Insects	800 000
Starfish, sea urchins etc.	6 000
Fishes	20 000
Amphibians, reptiles	8 500
Birds	8 600
Mammals	4 000
Plants	
Seaweeds etc.	9 000
Lichens	18 000
Mosses etc.	23 000
Ferns	10 000
Conifers etc.	600
Flowering plants	286 000
Fungi	40 000
Microorganisms	66 000
TOTAL	1 659 700

small fraction of all the species that have ever existed. Rates of speciation (the origin of species) and extinction (the death of species) vary considerably, and the evolutionary pathway is marked by a series of steep rises and falls (fig 3.3). Steep falls are termed mass extinctions. They are thought to occur as a result of catastrophic environmental change and are generally followed by a burst of speciation in which vacated niches are refilled. Perhaps the most dramatic of these mass extinctions involved the disappearance of the dinosaurs in the late Cretaceous period about 65 million years ago. A possible explanation of this is a 'nuclear winter' scenario following intense meteorite activity, although this is still a matter of great debate.

Over recent years we are witnessing another drop in biological diversity, this time as a result of human activity. The scale of extinction of the larger high-profile creatures, such as birds and mammals, has been well documented. In the last 300 years at least 200 forms have been lost, two-thirds being full species. Examples are given at the end of the chapters. The absence of a complete species list makes it difficult to establish the overall

Ratio of temperate and tropical species. The number of species in temperate regions is fairly well documented for most groups, whereas in tropical regions only the birds and mammals have been studied in detail. It has been found that there are 2–3 times as many tropical birds and mammals as temperate ones. It is therefore assumed that all other tropical groups are 2–3 times as numerous. An overall estimate based on this ratio puts the figure between 3 and 5 million.

Host-specific species. This estimate is based on a study of insects by Erwin in 1982. He collected more than 1200 species of beetles from the canopy of one species of tree in Panama and made the assumption that 13.5% were host-specific (only found on the tree species under study). Since beetles represent about 40% of all arthropods there must be about 400 host-specific species of arthropods in the canopy, and since canopy arthropods are twice as numerous as forest floor ones the total number of host-specific species of arthropods for the study tree is 600. Using an estimate of 50 000 tree species he concluded that there were approximately 30 million tropical arthropod species alone.

Length and species number. For species over 10 mm there is a linear relationship between log (length) and log (number of species) (fig 3.1). Below 10 mm this relationship breaks down. It is argued, though, that our knowledge of the smaller creatures is far from complete. Studies on parasites, for example, have been limited to humans and economically important host species. If every species was host to at least one specific parasite then the relationship might also apply below 10 mm. Extrapolation of the graph to 5 mm places the total species figure at over 10 million (fig. 3.1).

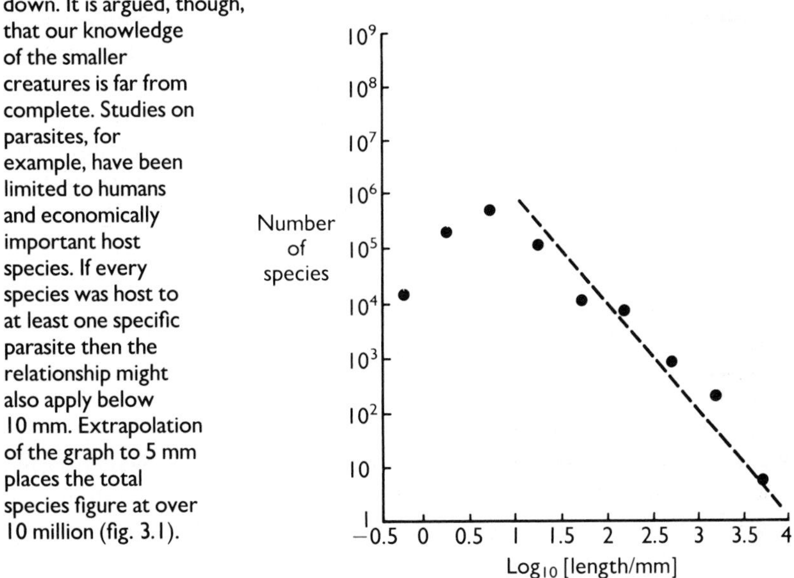

Fig 3.1 Relationship between length and number of species (from R.M. May, How many species are there on earth?, *Science*, **241**, 1981, 1441–9).

Predictions based on the above methods vary widely. Each has used fairly crude assumptions which may not be true. Erwin's estimate is dependent on the assumption that 13.5% of arthropods are host-specific. If he had chosen a value of 5% a revised estimate would be about 11 million. The last method is also highly speculative and highlights the problems of extrapolation, especially with a log scale. If the line was continued to include all sizes down to 1 mm, that is log (length) = 0, the total species number would be 100 million. Despite these difficulties it would be fair to conclude that there are significantly more species alive than have yet been recorded, particularly in the smaller groups.

Box 3.1 How many species?

Species	Subspecies	
lion (*Panthera leo*)	11	
tiger (*Panthera tigris*)	8	Bali tiger (*P.t.balica*) extinct c.1937 Caspian tiger (*P.t.virgata*) extinct c.1980 Javan tiger (*P.t.sondaica*) extinct c.1988 Siberian tiger (*P.t.altaica*) 500 Indo–Chinese tiger (*P.t.corbetti*) 2000 Sumatran tiger (*P.t.sumatrae*) 500 Indian tiger (*P.t.tigris*) 4000 Chinese tiger (*P.t.amoyensis*) 250
jaguar (*Panthera onca*)	8	
leopard (*Panthera pardus*)	15	

Fig 3.2 Variety within a species. Many species, especially those which occupy a wide geographic range, are made up of distinct subspecies or races. This can be seen in four species of big cats (genus *Panthera*). The status of each tiger subspecies is given alongside the name (from D. Day, *The Encyclopaedia of Vanished Species*, Hong Kong, McLaren, 1989).

extinction rate. The matter is further complicated by the high levels of diversity and endemism (that is species confined to one region) in the areas which are under the greatest threat, namely the tropics. Nevertheless, there is general agreement that species are currently being lost at the rate of several species per day and that by the end of the century this rate will climb to several species per hour. In addition, many species have been genetically eroded (box 3.2). That is their gene pool has become reduced and with it the capacity to adapt. Without this ability their status is seriously threatened.

Human activity

A wide range of human activities are responsible for the decline in biodiversity and these are discussed below.

Habitat destruction This is the major cause of current losses. It is inextricably linked to human population growth and an insatiable demand for resources. In 1987 the world population passed the 5 billion mark. The World Bank estimates that this number will rise to 11 billion before reaching a plateau in c.2150. Population growth is not uniform throughout the world (table 3.2). In developed countries population growth has reached the plateau phase (box 3.3), and much of the natural vegetation has already been lost. In Britain, for example, the climax vegetation, temperate forest, now accounts for just 9% of the land area. In the USA, the prairies, which once covered 1 million sq km are now confined to 16 000 sq km of Kansas (that is 2% of the original).

In developing countries population growth is still in the exponential phase and destruction of vegetation is at a peak. Clearance on the same scale as in developed countries, however, would have far more damaging consequences because of the high levels of diversity and endemism in the species found there, as previously mentioned.

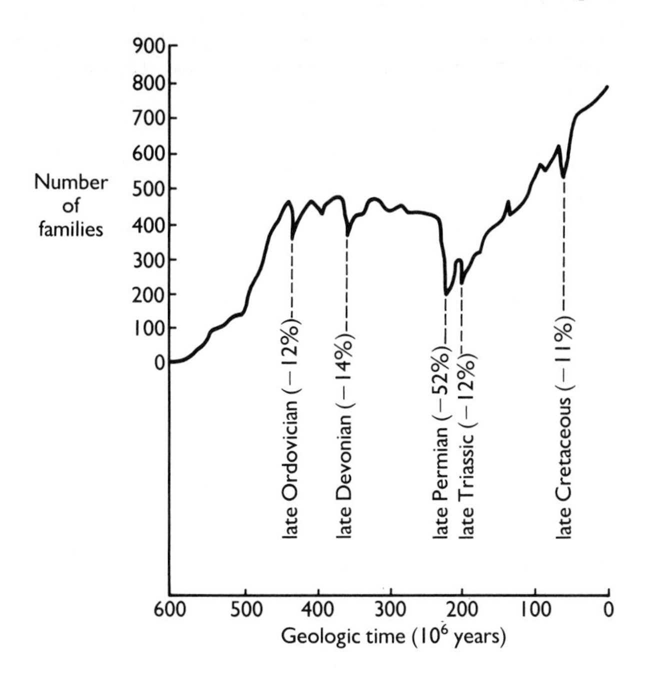

Fig 3.3 The pattern of speciation and extinction in the fossil record. Five mass extinctions are recognized. The relative losses are given in parentheses (from D.M. Raup and J.J. Seposki, Mass extinctions in the marine fossil record, *Science*, **215**, 1982, 1501–3).

Tropical rainforests These cover just 7% of the land surface but are home to at least 50% of all living species. Tropical forests once covered 15 million sq km but are now reduced to 9 million sq km; a loss of 40%. Current losses are conservatively estimated to be about 76 000 sq km per year. (To give you some idea of the extent of this loss, Britain has an area of 244 000 sq km.) If deforestation continued at this rate the world's tropical forests would be cleared in 120 years. Exponential population growth, however, seems set to speed up this loss. Satellite images of Rhondonia, a southern state of Brazil, reveal a dramatic increase in cleared forest in a period that population has risen rapidly (fig 3.6).

Studies on species–area relationships have suggested, not surprisingly, that as an area gets smaller it supports fewer species. The exact relationship varies from ecosystem to ecosystem and not enough is known yet to relate this to tropical rainforests. It is certain though that losses have already occurred and that if deforestation continues unchecked the number of extinctions will be considerable.

As well as being the habitat containing the greatest variety of species, tropical forests also have an important role in ecological processes. On a local level they regulate the water cycle and protect the fragile soil. On a

The characteristics of an organism are coded for by **genes**. These are discrete lengths of DNA which occupy fixed positions on chromosomes (fig 3.4).

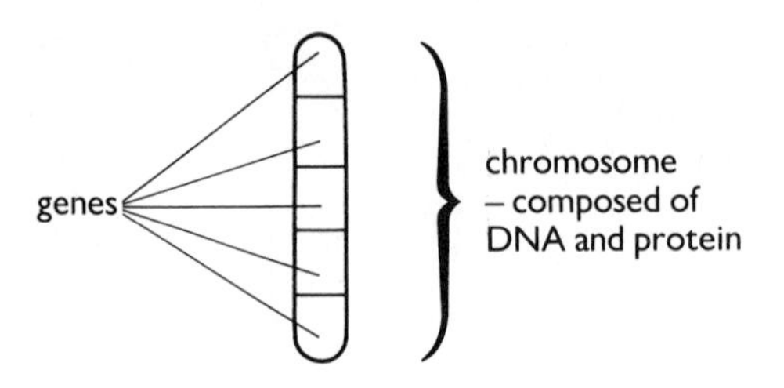

Fig 3.4

For each characteristic there may be several alternative forms called **alleles**. The gene for coat colour in the rabbit, for example, has four alleles: agouti (grey/brown), chinchilla (grey/black), himalayan (white with black extremities – nose, ears, feet and tail) and albino (white). The term **gene pool** is rather misleading. It actually means the sum total of alleles in the population. Similarly, **genetic erosion** refers to the loss of alleles from a population.

Box 3.2 Gene pools and genetic erosion.

global level they are a massive store of fixed carbon. Unless the present trend of forest loss is arrested host countries face ecological disaster as a result of soil erosion and the carbon dioxide that is liberated by burning has menacing implications for global climate.

Hunting Years ago when humans were hunter–gatherers, low population levels and relatively crude weapons meant that we had little impact on food chains. Today, overpopulation and sophisticated weaponry have placed species under increasing pressure. This pressure was too great in some cases. Among the most famous examples are the dodo and passenger pigeon. The first became a victim of its adaptive radiation: years of island life without predators rendered the dodo flightless and easy prey for hungry sailors. Predictable flight patterns made the low-flying passenger pigeon vulnerable to high-flying buckshot. The rest, as they say, is history. Lesser-known examples of animals hunted to extinction include bluebuck (an African antelope), aurochs (a European wild ox) and quagga (a subspecies of zebra).

A more responsible attitude by nations over their larger wildlife has lessened the chances of history repeating. Hunting for food has now been largely replaced by the farm, abbatoir and supermarket. Hunting for sport is still fairly widespread, although the 'game' is often supplemented by artificially reared animals. This is not the case in Italy where about 200 million native and migrating birds are shot annually (for 'sport'?).

Species which inhabit international waters are still very vulnerable. Advanced echo location of shoals mean that fish catches are massive. The

Table 3.2 *World population statistics (from the* World Population Data Sheet, *Population Reference Bureau, Washington DC, 1987).*

Country	*Population (millions)* 1987	2020	*Births (per 1000)*	*Deaths (per 1000)*	*Per capita GNP (US$)*
USA	243.8	296.6	16	9	16 400
Japan	122.2	122.9	12	6	11 330
UK	56.8	56.6	13	12	8 390
India	800.3	1310	33	12	250
China	1062	1361	21	8	310
Brazil	141.5	233.8	29	8	1 640
Indonesia	174.9	284.2	31	10	530
Cameroon	10.3	23.5	43	16	810
Kenya	22.4	79.2	52	13	290

A typical population growth curve of a species with a sustained food supply and a small number of founding individuals is sigmoid in shape (fig 3.5). Human population growth can be divided into three phases:

I **Lag phase**: Population growth is slow. Birth rates are high, but so too are death rates.
II **Exponential phase**: Population growth is rapid. Birth rates are high, but death rates have been reduced as a result of improvements in nutrition, medicine and hygiene.
III **Plateau phase**: Population growth has stabilized. Birth rates have been reduced due to family planning, and death rates are low.

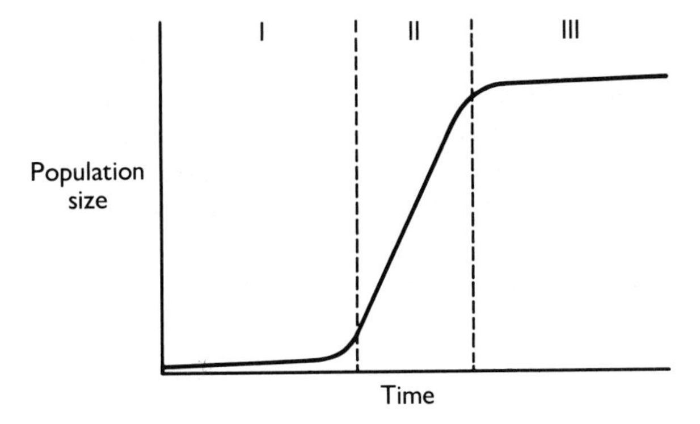

Fig 3.5 Population growth curve.

The world human population is currently in the exponential phase. Such a growth rate creates an ever-increasing demand for living space, food, energy and minerals. As a result natural vegetation and its associated fauna is displaced and depleted.

Box 3.3 Population growth.

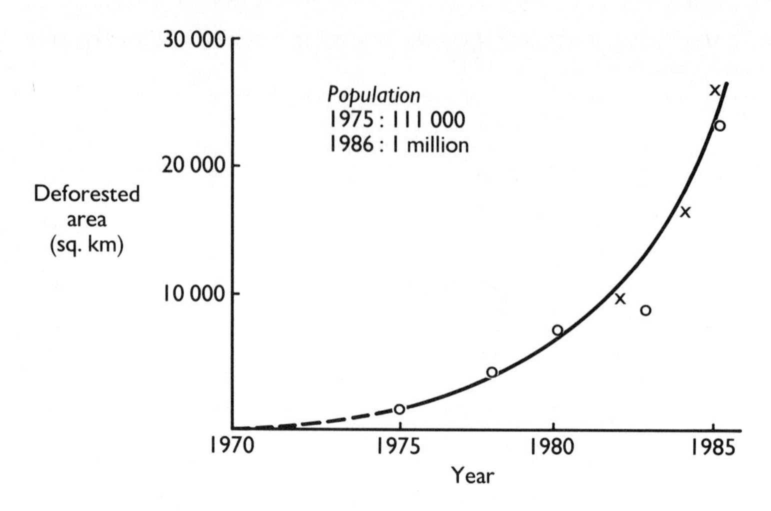

Fig 3.6 Deforestation in Rhondonia. x = data from satellite images, o = ground-based estimates. If the exponential rate of increase in deforestation continues, it is estimated that complete clearance will occur by the year 2000 (from J. Malingreau & C.J. Tucker, Large-scale deforestation in the southeastern Amazon Basin of Brazil, *Ambio*, **17**(1), 1988, 49–55).

imposition of quotas and mesh-size net limitations in European waters have provided temporary relief, but in other areas hunting continues unchecked. In the Pacific, drift nets up to 30 km long catch squid and salmon in the north and tuna in the south. This practice, aptly named the 'wall of death', also traps other marine animals such as turtles, dolphins, seals, sealions and small whales.

Sophisticated technology has also spelt danger for the great whales. Whalers equipped with harpoon cannons and attendant factory ships have systematically hunted species to the verge of extinction (fig 3.7). Their endangered status is compounded by low reproductive potential and poor powers of recovery. Despite the efforts of the International Whaling Commission some nations, notably Japan and Norway, continue to hunt for research purposes, although the value of this is not always clear (see section 4.6).

Trade Wildlife and their products have traditionally been used for clothes ornament, superstition, medicine and pets. They represent a resource with enormous economic potential. Table 3.3 gives the current value of some species and products. International trade is thought to be worth about $5 billion annually and threatens many species with extinction. The most traded species and products are given in table 3.4. They are typically exported from the developing countries of Central and South America, Africa and Asia to the developed nations of North America, Europe and the Far East. CITES (the Convention on International Trade in Endangered Species) estimates that each year trade affects about:

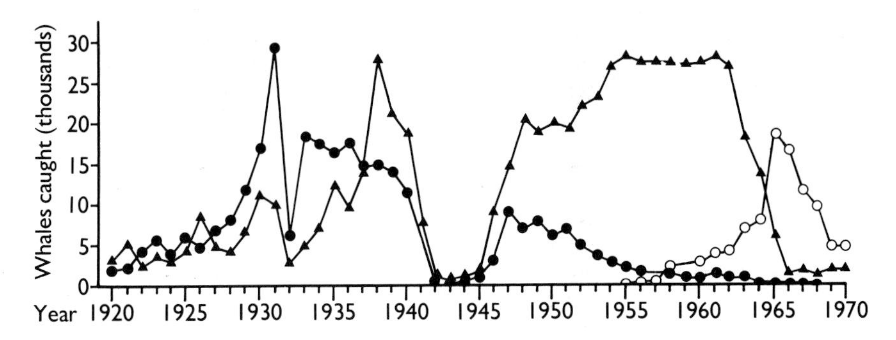

Fig 3.7 Decline in catches of blue, fin and sei whales (from J.A. Gulland, The effect of exploitation on the numbers of marine animals. *Proceedings for the Advance Study Institute for Dynamics Numbers Population*, Oosterbeck, 1970, 450–68).

40 000 primates
1million orchids
3 million live birds
10 million reptile skins
15 million furs
>350 million tropical fishes

Some species get caught in a downward spiral of supply and demand. Dwindling numbers make the product less available which increases the price and encourages more intense hunting. This phenomenon is particularly evident in the trade in parrots. The attractiveness of these birds has caused several species to be collected to the verge of extinction. Similarly, the future of the African elephant (*Loxodonta africana*) seems closely linked to the ivory trade (see section 4.5), while the black rhino (*Diceros bicornis*) and black bear (*Ursus americanus*) owe their plight to the demands of oriental medicine. Rhino horn is thought to cure rheumatism, paralysis, fever and epilepsy while black bear gall bladder is prescribed for liver, stomach and intestinal complaints.

Introduced species Ecosystems evolve over long periods of time during which a balance develops between the various members of the communities involved. Each occupies a niche in which it can secure enough food to grow and reproduce. Occasionally new species may appear and compete with niche holders. This may occur naturally, such as when the land bridge formed linking North and South America for the first time. In the competition that ensued the marsupial mammals of the southern continent were driven to extinction by the eutherian mammals from the north. Deliberate introductions by humans have set off similar struggles.

Table 3.3 *Current value of some species and their products.*

Species/Product	*Value (US$)*	*Source*
Ivory	260/kg	S. Armstrong & F. Bridgland (1989)
Rhino horn	3 600/kg	C. Joyce (1989)
Black bear gall bladder	10 000/kg	C. Joyce (1989)
Palm cockatoo	16 000 each	J. Holm (1989)
Panda skin	25 000 each	CITES secretariat (1990)
Slipper orchid	3 500 each	CITES secretariat (1990)

C. Joyce, Dying to get on the list, *New Scientist*, 30.9.89, 42–7.
S. Armstrong & F. Bridgland, Elephants and the ivory tower, *New Scientist*, 26.8.89, 37–41.
J. Holm, Polly wants a crackdown, *BBC Wildlife*, July 1989, 430–6.

Table 3.4 *Most traded species and products (from CITES secretariat (Doc.0042Z, pp. 1–18, 1990)).*

Taxa	*Live organisms*	*Products*
mammals	primates	leather and furs
		ivory
birds	geese and ducks	stuffed birds
	raptors	ostrich (skin and meat)
	parrots and budgerigars	eggs
	hummingbirds	
	passerines	
reptiles	snakes and lizards	sea turtles (shells and soup)
	tortoises	crocodile and lizard skins
	sea turtles	
amphibians		frogs' legs
fishes	tropical fish	
invertebrates	leeches	mounted butterflies
	spiders	corals
plants	orchids	
	cacti	

Island communities are very vulnerable to introductions. Often an island may be colonized by vegetation, insects and birds but is unreachable by mammals. Adaptive evolution may then lead to the evolution of flightlessness. European settlers to Hawaii introduced domestic animals and predators such as cats, rats and mongooses. These almost certainly contributed to the extinction of 24 of the islands' 70 known endemic species and subspecies.

War This can have a devastating effect on wildlife, particularly evident in Vietnam (1964–73). It has been estimated that 22 000 sq km of forest and farmland, and 1240 sq km of mangroves, were destroyed as a result of bombing, mechanized land clearance, defoliation and napalming. 25 million bomb craters were formed, some up to 30 m in diameter, and the herbicides that were used, including the infamous 'agent orange', were highly persistent and are still found in high levels in the soil and wildlife.

Pollution Another consequence of overpopulation is the production of a wide range of pollutants. Pollutants, by definition, are toxic to wildlife but the extent of their harm is related to a number of factors. These include the toxicity of the pollutant, the extent of the pollution and the persistence of the pollutant. The effects of four types of pollution will be considered.

1. *Eutrophication*, the nutrient enrichment of natural waters, results from a number of sources. Human sewage together with leachate from agricultural systems (containing animal sewage, silage liquor and inorganic fertilizers) lead to increased levels of organic matter, nitrates and phosphates. These trigger algal blooms which reduce light penetration, killing submerged aquatic plants. When the algae die they provide a substrate for decomposers which in turn leads to deoxygenation and loss of aquatic animals. If the enrichment resulted from a single incident the nutrients would be degraded and the community would recover fairly quickly. Continuous enrichment, however, can lead to long-term deoxygenation of the water with serious consequences for native organisms.
2. *Oil* is a particularly toxic pollutant which causes the blanket destruction of wildlife. Oil spillages from holed tankers can affect extensive areas. In 1989 the Exxon Valdez leaked 240 000 barrels of crude oil into the waters of Alaska's Prince William Sound. It covered 60 000 sq km of sea and shoreline. It is reasonable to suppose that pollution affecting such large areas would threaten species with restricted ranges, as well as seriously reducing numbers of more widespread species.
3. *Pesticides* are typically highly toxic, non-specific and persistent. Consequently, they not only remove the unwanted organisms, but destroy other related species and become trapped in food chains. DDT is a well-documented pesticide. It is an organochlorine insecticide which had widespread use in the 1950s. Clear Lake in California was treated with DDT in 1949, 1954 and 1957 to kill midges. The DDT was found to accumulate in the food chain and led to breeding failure in the grebes on the lake between 1950 and 1962. DDT and its derivatives were also responsible for the decline of some birds of prey. In the European sparrowhawk (*Accipiter nisus*) the insecticide was found to interfere with calcium metabolism leading to egg shell thinning and breeding failure.
4. *Greenhouse effect*: Some gases, including carbon dioxide and methane trap reradiated heat from the Earth's surface and may lead to atmospheric warming. The Earth's climate results from the interaction of a large number of factors and naturally undergoes periodic change but if, as is feared, greenhouse gases lead to rises in temperature over a short period of time it will pose a serious threat. Some species have evolved to operate within very narrow physiological limits. Without time to adjust they would quickly perish.

Many pollution incidents are single localized events. In the case of biodegradable pollutants the environment is normally able to facilitate a recovery with little threat to species. Persistent pollutants, however, are more likely to lead to extinctions.

Indigenous peoples

Indigenous people are also threatened by modern human activity. Evidence suggests that until about 10 000 years ago most humans were hunter–gatherers. From that period the discovery, by some, of agriculture laid the foundation for modern human society.

A few hunter–gatherer societies still exist (fig 3.8), although their status is far from secure. The Waorani Indians of Eastern Ecuador, for example, are seeing their environment degraded by colonists and uncontrolled oil exploitation. The Yanomami Indians, the largest surviving tribe in Brazil, are threatened by the invasion of gold miners. Numbers have fallen drastically as a result of mercury poisoning, used in the extraction of gold, and diseases brought by the miners.

3.2 The value of nature

The reasons for stopping the current loss of biological diversity fall into four main categories: ethical, aesthetic, utilitarian and ecological.

Ethical

The fact that you are reading this book probably indicates a certain interest in the natural world. Therefore, although you might have difficulty in expressing the reason, you would probably consider that it was wrong to make a species extinct. Morality is an abstract concept though. It is largely moulded by our social environment, particularly the prevailing religious and political beliefs, and thus the question of right and wrong will vary from culture to culture. Despite the changing nature of morality, it is a useful exercise to construct a defence against the loss of species on these grounds. Have a go now, before reading further.

Included in your argument might be the claim that organisms have an intrinsic value that is greater than the one we have given. That is creatures have an unquestionable right to existence, a view taken for example by the UN World Charter for Nature (p. 14). Counter to this opinion is the fact that extinction, as we have seen, is a natural phenomenon. The fossil record is littered with the petrified remains of lost species. Further, if all life forms have a right to existence how should we relate to pathogenic species? A lot of human suffering could be prevented if, for example, the smallpox virus and malarial *Plasmodium* were eradicated.

You might also consider that the natural world is a human heritage that should be preserved intact for the generations to come, although this has a

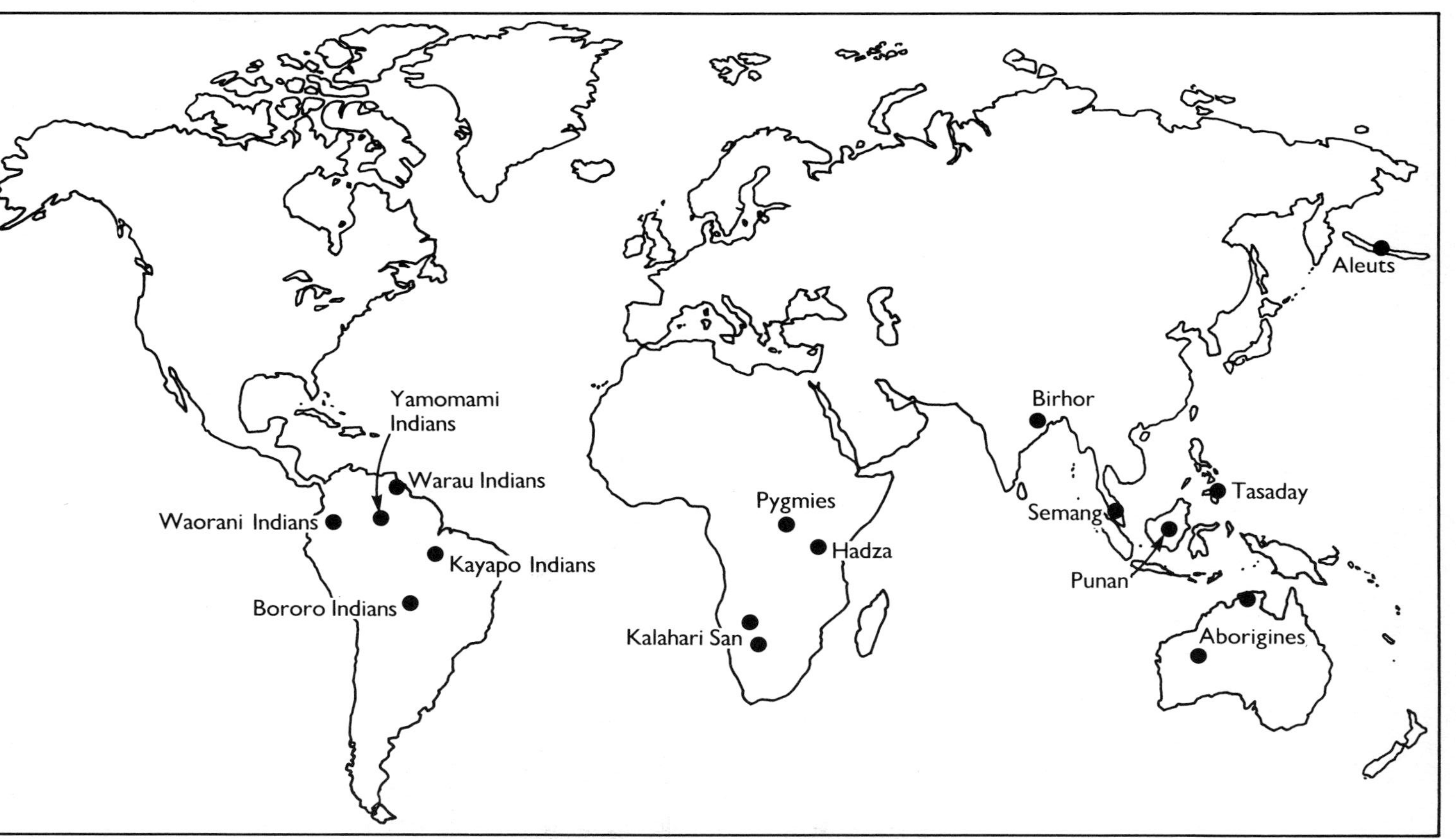

Fig 3.8 Some hunter-gatherer societies still in existence (from R. Leakey, *The Making of Mankind*, Michael Joseph, 1981).

utilitarian aspect to it. It is a far easier task to objectively defend wildlife anthropocentrically (from a human viewpoint). The remaining categories fall into this classification.

Aesthetic

Aesthetic is defined as that which is pleasing to behold. We are able to derive great enjoyment from our natural environment. The shapes, colours, textures and movement of wildlife stimulates our senses and enriches our culture. Plants and animals undoubtedly affect the quality of our lives. This may be related to times past when we were more dependent on them for our survival. Glimpses of extant hunter–gatherer societies give us a reminder of how intimate we all once were with 'Mother Earth'. This association is manifest in the popularity of zoos, museums and botanic gardens and our use of the countryside as a recreational facility. In a survey carried out by the Countryside Commission of England and Wales in 1978 54% of the population visited the countryside during that summer.

Our appreciation of the beauty and fascination of wildlife is also illustrated by the myriad of organizations which exist to protect different organisms. In Britain there are about 750 000 members of the Royal Society for the Protection of Birds, all united by their shared concern for our feathered friends.

Wildlife is also a popular subject for film makers. The BBC1 programme *Wildlife on One* on 29.1.81 attracted an audience of 15 million. Natural history programmes are now a regular feature in the TV schedules.

Utilitarian

Wildlife contributes to our material well-being in a number of ways.

Agriculture We depend on the photosynthetic ability of plants to convert the sun's energy into a consumable form. It has been estimated that of the 250 000 species of higher plants 3000 have been used for food at one time or another. Of these just 30 species currently account for 95% of human nutrition (fig 3.9).

Large-scale monocultivation of high-cropping varieties leads to problems from pest attack. This was clearly demonstrated by the catastrophic potato blight in Ireland in the 1840s. From a human population of eight million, two million starved to death while a further two million emigrated. A more recent example of the vulnerability of a monoculture involved corn in the USA in 1970. 15% of the entire American corn crop was destroyed by a leaf fungus. No-one starved as a result but the losses were reckoned to be about $2 billion.

The solution to pestilence on this scale is to search for a wild relative or primitive cultivar that is naturally resistant to the pest. The desired genes from the new stock are then incorporated into the crop plant by a careful process of cross-breeding and screening.

Within a species there is a considerable amount of genetic diversity which is manifest in a wide range of forms. All exist by virtue of the fact that they have evolved the necessary alleles (alternate forms of a gene) to cope with their environment. These alleles include those responsible for characteristics offering defence against would-be pests. Consequently, there is a strong probability that out there somewhere, by virtue of its existence, a strain of the crop plant has already solved the pest problem. At least this was the case until recently. The wild relatives of the major crop species are mostly to be found in the tropical regions which as we have seen are being eroded at an alarming rate.

In the same way that different strains have achieved immunity from disease, so too have they conquered such problems as low light levels, high salinity, low nutrient levels and extremes of temperature. With selective

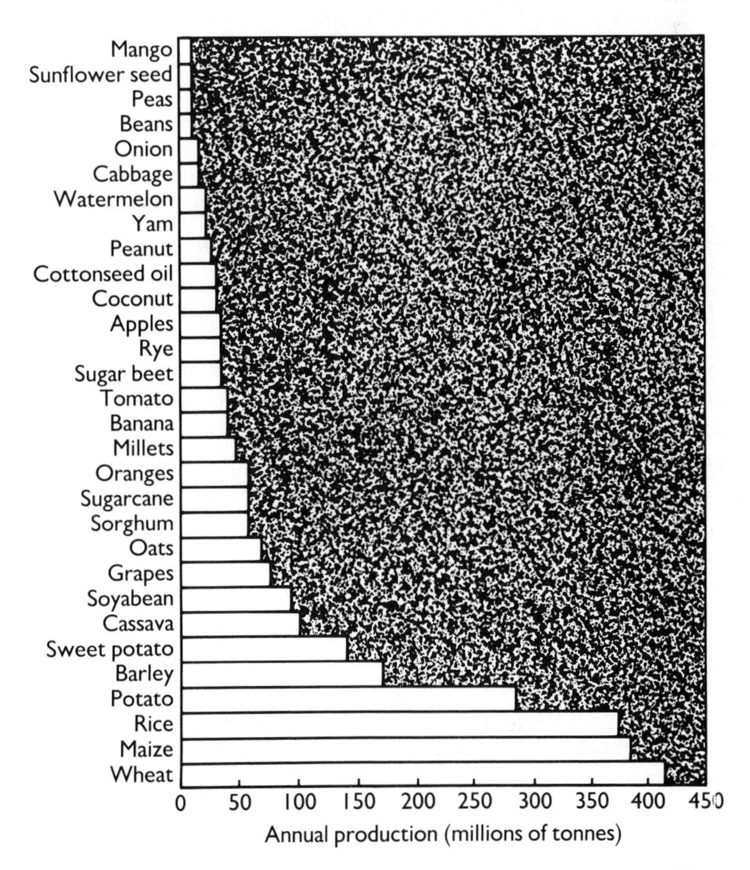

Fig 3.9 Annual production of the major crop plants (from O. Sattaur, The shrinking gene pool, *New Scientist*, 29.7.89, 37–41).

breeding the potential exists to create productive strains which could be grown in those marginal areas that will have to be brought into cultivation to support the ever-growing human population.

Similarly, stock animals which are reared in high density are vulnerable to disease and pestilence. They too may be made resistant by incorporating genes from wild relatives.

Medicine Despite the apparent differences between plants and animals they share a large number of metabolic pathways. As a result plants produce a wide range of compounds within their tissues which are of considerable medicinal benefit to humans (table 3.5). The world value of plant-derived prescription drugs was estimated in 1982 to be about $40 billion. These drugs were predominantly derived from only 41 species which had been selected from the analysis of 5000 species. Considering that there is a world total of 250 000 higher plants, the potential exists for a whole range of new drugs.

Developing countries are even more reliant on plant-derived drugs. China and India utilize 1700 and 2500 species respectively.

Plants and animals undergo a similar process of cell division and are therefore both prone to the disturbances in the cell cycle which lead to tumour formation. Not surprisingly some plants possess anti-cancer properties. The most celebrated in this respect is the rosy periwinkle (*Catharanthus roseus*) from Madagascar. Two alkaloids obtained from the plant, vincristine and vinblastine, have dramatically improved the treatment of Hodgkins' disease, a form of lymphatic cancer, and some types of leukaemia. Remission from Hodgkins' disease has increased from 19% to 80% and remission from acute lymphocytic leukaemia is now at 99%. It is thought that up to one in ten plants possess anti-cancer properties. Only a small percentage of the flora has been screened, which means that a potential solution may exist, as yet undiscovered, for this dreaded disease.

Animals contribute to medicine in a number of ways. They may be a source of drugs. Animal-derived drugs include alantoin from blowfly larvae which promotes deep healing of wounds, hirudin from leeches which serves as a blood anticoagulant and bee venom which is used in the treatment of arthritis.

Animals also serve as models for human physiology and may help in the understanding of physiological processes. The giant squid (*Architeuthis* sp.) for example possesses a giant axon which provides a more manageable system for the investigation of nerve action. Animals may serve as a model for the treatment of disease. It has been found that the armadillo (*Dasypus* spp.) and the Mangabey monkey (*Cercocebus* sp.) also suffer from leprosy, and that the springbok (*Antidorcas* sp.) suffers from polycystic disease of the kidney. The presence of these afflictions in non-humans provides an alternative option for research. Some animals may, as a result of their unique physiology, offer a clue in the understanding of some human ailments. The bison (*Bison bison*) for example, does not appear to suffer

Table 3.5 *Major plant contributors to medicine (from N. Myers,* A Wealth of Wild Species, *Storehouse for Human Welfare, Westview, 1983).*

Plant	*Drug*	*Use*
Purple foxglove (*Digitalis purpurea*)	digitalis	cardiac stimulant
Grecian foxglove (*Digitalis lanata*)	digoxin	cardiac stimulant
Serpentine root (*Rauwolfia serpentina*)	reserpine	tranquilliser
Cephaelis ipecacuanha	ipecac	amoebic dysentery
Ephedra sp.	ephedrine	nasal decongestant and nerve stimulant
Rosy periwinkle (*Catharanthus roseus*)	vincristine and vinblastine	anti-cancer
Mexican yam (*Dioscorea mexicana*)	diosgenin	base for the synthesis of oral contraceptives, cortisone and hydrocortisone

from cancer. Isolation of the factors responsible would greatly promote research in this field.

Industry We have been reliant on plants and animals for material goods since the origin of our species. The twentieth century has seen the introduction of increasing numbers of synthetic alternatives but plants, in particular, are still widely used in many industrial processes.

Trees of course provide timber. This still plays a major role in the construction industry and it is used in the production of furniture, as fuel and as pulp for paper production. Plants also provide a range of compounds from their tissues. These include rubber, oils, waxes, resins, gums, dyes, cellulose, starch and hydrocarbons.

Rubber, oil and wax are in great demand. Inferior alternatives to the first two can be artificially synthesised from petrochemicals, but as geological oil reserves decline the role of plants as provider seems set to gain in importance. The search is now on for new and more productive species.

Plant biomass may be used for the production of energy. It can be digested anaerobically to produce biogas (carbon dioxide and methane), or fermented to produce ethanol or pyrolised (thermally decomposed in the absence of oxygen) to produce hydrocarbons. Ethanol has been combined with petrol to form gasohol, a fuel which can be used in motor vehicles. Hydrocarbons have properties which resemble crude petroleum. Some plants of the euphorbia family actually produce hydrocarbons instead of carbohydrates. These have the advantage over drilled oil of being sulphur-free.

Ecological

The presence of plant and animal communities serve humans indirectly. They maintain the integrity of the environment by regulating ecological cycles such as water, carbon and nitrogen. Undisturbed these various cycles remain relatively stable. The plant-dominated ecosystems represent a massive store of fixed carbon but as the vegetation is removed or burnt, this stabilizing effect is lost. The resulting liberation of carbon dioxide together with emissions from the combustion of fossil fuels have created conditions which may lead to global warming.

The presence of vegetation also stabilizes the soil and protects it from the physical impact of the weather. This role was graphically illustrated by events in Thailand in November 1988: 450 people died and 40 000 were made homeless as a result of flooding and landslides that were attributable to deforestation.

Individual organisms, particularly in the upper trophic levels, unwittingly act as pollution monitors. The breeding failure of birds of prey in the 1960s, for example, drew attention to the persistent and toxic properties of DDT. Lichens are found to be sensitive to air pollution, particularly sulphur dioxide.

Species may be called on as the agents of biological pest control. The introduction of alien species either deliberately or by accident can sometimes have devastating consequences. The prickly pear cactus (*Opuntia* spp.), for example, was introduced to Australia from South America in 1900 as a hedging plant. By 1952, however, it had covered 24 million ha of grazing land. Biological control involves importing the natural predator or parasite of the pest, in this case the larva of the moth *Cactoblastis*. This was obtained from Argentina and quickly brought the prickly pear under control.

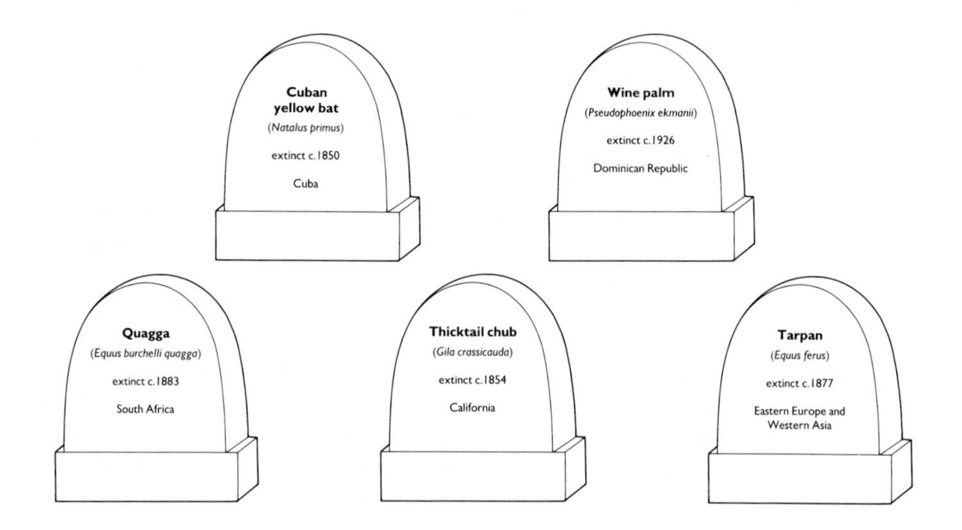

4

Conservation in practice

It would be unrealistic to think that conservation is all gloom and doom. On the contrary, and thanks to the goodwill and enthusiasm of many people throughout the world, there are many exciting and encouraging success stories in biological conservation. It is for this reason that we have decided to fill the main section of this book with examples of conservation in practice. The range of topics is not comprehensive but it is wide and varied so as to reflect the breadth and importance of biological conservation.

As in previous sections we have deliberately included some specific suggestions for further reading in the bibliography at the end of the book. Although some of these references would appear to be of a specialist nature, many are books (available in local libraries) and some are scientific journals which are available at centres of higher education.

4.1 Taxonomy, systematics and biodatabases: the keys to biological conservation

Taxonomy, the oldest and most fundamental of all the biological sciences, is concerned with the study, description, naming and classification of organisms. **Systematics** refers to the classification of living organisms into groups and the relationships between those groups. Taxonomy provides a basic service to biology and is also a key to successful biological conservation.

No one really knows how many species there are living today but estimates range from 5 million to in excess of 30 million. After more than 200 years of study by taxonomists, only about 1.7 million species have been described and fewer have been studied in depth. There are many reasons why we need to identify species. For example, before adequate conservation measures can be undertaken, it is necessary to make an accurate identification of the species. The many species as yet unnamed may be a source of chemicals and genetic material which could be used for improving varieties of crop plants and for biological control of pests and diseases. Also, the vast array of plants and animals as yet not studied in depth may be a source of materials which could be used in medicine.

The basis of taxonomy and systematics

Animals and plants are named and classified on the basis of various features and characteristics and we owe much to the Swedish biologist Carl Linné (Linnaeus) who, in the mid to late 1800s, gave us a basic binomial system for classifying organisms. All organisms, when identified, are given a binomial name which is made of the generic and specific name, for example *Felis catus* (domestic cat) and *Felis silvestris* (wild cat). Closely related genera are grouped into **families**, the groups of families make up an **order**, the orders are grouped into a **class** and the classes into a **phylum**.

Why do we need an international classification system? First, it is a kind of filing system for all the names, and secondly, the hierarchical system also provides a basis for classifying as yet unnamed species, for studying relationships between species and the study of evolution. To be able to identify and refer to an animal or plant we require a name which is consistently meaningful and internationally recognized. After all, although the vernacular names ungurawe, majo, isan and hara are very familiar to local people in parts of Peru, it is only the scientific name *Jessenia bataua* which could lead people from other countries to understand that the plant being referred to, in this case, is one with fruits which can be made into drinks with medicinal properties.

Taxonomists draw on more than just external characters or structural information for the identification and classification of plants and animals. As well as morphological and anatomical information, information from chromosomes and also many chemicals found in the organisms are used in taxonomy. It is partly because taxonomists deal with a wide range of information (including geographical distribution, anatomical features, behaviour and chemical compounds) that their skills have made important contributions not only to taxonomy but also to identification of useful chemicals and other materials.

Biodatabases

Collections of information or databases, which include the vernacular and scientific names of species as well as descriptions, provide a basis for classification of species. Databases of this kind of information can be extended to include data on the biology and ecology of various species. What use can we make of biodatabases or these computer-based collections of information? Imagine, for example, you were looking for new species and varieties of fruits and vegetables which could be grown in arid areas where fresh water for irrigation is scarce. Where would you start to look for information? The amount of information could be vast because searches for genetic material in wild forms to be used in the improvement of crop plants and grazing plants have been on-going since Mendelian times (1822–84) and the start of modern genetics. During that time an enormous amount of information on wild and cultivated plants has been collected and deposited in libraries and herbariums throughout the world. The amount of information on just one species can be large and scattered through many reports in different languages. One single source of information could be a biodatabase which provides taxonomic, genetic and ecological data about the wild forms of plants growing in dry or salty conditions. Such a database might tell you that there is a wild species of tomato growing on the Galapagos Islands (off the coast of Ecuador) which is salt-tolerant. Varieties (or cultivars) of that tomato are now grown in arid areas where irrigation uses saline water. Without the biodatabase, information about that tomato may have been difficult to find.

We depend on very few plant species (about 25–30) for the world's staple diets. We do, however, use many varieties of those few species and those varieties are bred and selected for having certain useful characteristics. The wild forms provide us with valuable genetic material which is used to improve the varieties of crop plants. There is, of course, more than just one species of wild wheat, potato, bean, and so on, and indeed in most cases there are many wild species, some of which have not been studied in any depth. It is essential to have a good biodatabase on plant genetic resources which can be used to systematically store, cross-reference and communicate information. In other words, what is needed is a database where all the available information on all these species can be stored then made available to those researching them. This is no easy task, even for those species which have been studied, because the information may be scattered amongst thousands of scientific journals and in dozens of languages. With modern computers and new technology, such a biodatabase might include illustrations as well as written information.

Some biodatabases are being designed to research alternative and better plant protein sources, such as might be found amongst leguminous plants. For example, a research group based at Kew Gardens, London and Southampton University has discovered new species of a relative of the broad bean, also low-toxin relatives of khesari dahl (grass pea) from Syria and, in addition, has rescued valuable genetic material from areas in Turkey which are to be flooded. Leguminous plants fix nitrogen from the atmosphere with the help of some bacteria on the plant's roots and there are about 18 000 species (about one-twelfth of all plant species) which include the group known as the Vicieae (wild relatives of lentils, peas and broad beans (box 4.1). These species have an important potential for improved food plants but there are many species of Vicieae which have yet to be described and named, let alone studied. The same can be said of the one genus *Phaseolus*, which includes some common beans, yet there is

Family Leguminosae

Sub-family Caesalpinioideae	Genera of particular economic and ecological interest
Tribe 1. Caesalpinieae	*Gleditsia, Caesalpinia* (Poinciana)
2. Cassieae	*Cassia, Senna, Ceratonia*
3. Cercideae	*Cercis, Bauhinia*
4. Detarieae	
5. Amherstieae	*Tamarindus, Julbernardia, Brachystegia, Isoberlinia*
Sub-family Mimosoideae	
Tribe 1. Parkieae	*Parkia*
2. Mimozygantheae	
3. Mimoseae	*Leucaena, Mimosa, Prosopis, Desmanthus*
4. Acacieae	*Acacia*
5. Ingeae	*Albizia, Inga, Pithecellobium, Samanea*
Sub-family Papilionoideae	
Tribe 1. Swartzieae	
2. Sophoreae	
3. Dipteryxeae	
4. Dalbergieae	
5. Abrus	*Abrus*
6. Tephrosieae	*Tephrosia, Derris, Lonchocarpus, Wisteria*
7. Robinieae	*Robinia, Gliricidia, Sesbania*
8. Indigoferae	*Indigofera, Cyamopsis*
9. Desmodieae	*Desmodium, Alysicarpus, Lespedeza*
10. Phaseoleae	*Phaseolus, Vigna,* etc.
11. Psoraleae	
12. Amorpheae	
13. Sesbanieae	
14. Aeschynomeneae	*Aeschynomene, Arachis, Stylosanthes, Zornia*
15. Adesmieae	*Adesmia*
16. Galegeae	*Galgea, Glycyrrhiza, Astragalus*
17. Carmichaelieae	
18. Hedysareae	*Hedysarum, Onobrychis*
19. Loteae	*Lotus, Anthyllis*
20. Coronilleae	*Coronilla, Ornithopus*
21. Vicieae	*Vicia, Lathyrus, Pisum, Lens*
22. Cicereae	*Cicer*
23. Trifolieae	*Trifolium, Medicago, Ononis, Melilotus*
24. Brongniartieae	
25. Mirbelieae	
26. Bossiaeae	
27. Podalyrieae	
28. Liparieae	*Cytisus, Ulex, Spartium*
29. Crotalarieae	*Crotalaria, Lotonois*
30. Euchresteae	
31. Thermopsideae	
32. Genisteae	*Genista, Lupinus, Laburnum*

⇩

Genus *Phaseolus* L.
Section *Phaseolus*

1 *Phaseolus vulgaris* L. common bean, French bean, haricot, navy bean, pole bean etc.
- var. *vulgaris*
- var. *aborigineus*

2 *Phaseolus coccineus* L. Scarlet runner bean (red flowered), butter bean (white flowered)
- ssp. *coccineus*
- ssp. *obvallatus*
- ssp. *formosus*
- ssp. *polyanthus*

3 *Phaseolus glabellus*

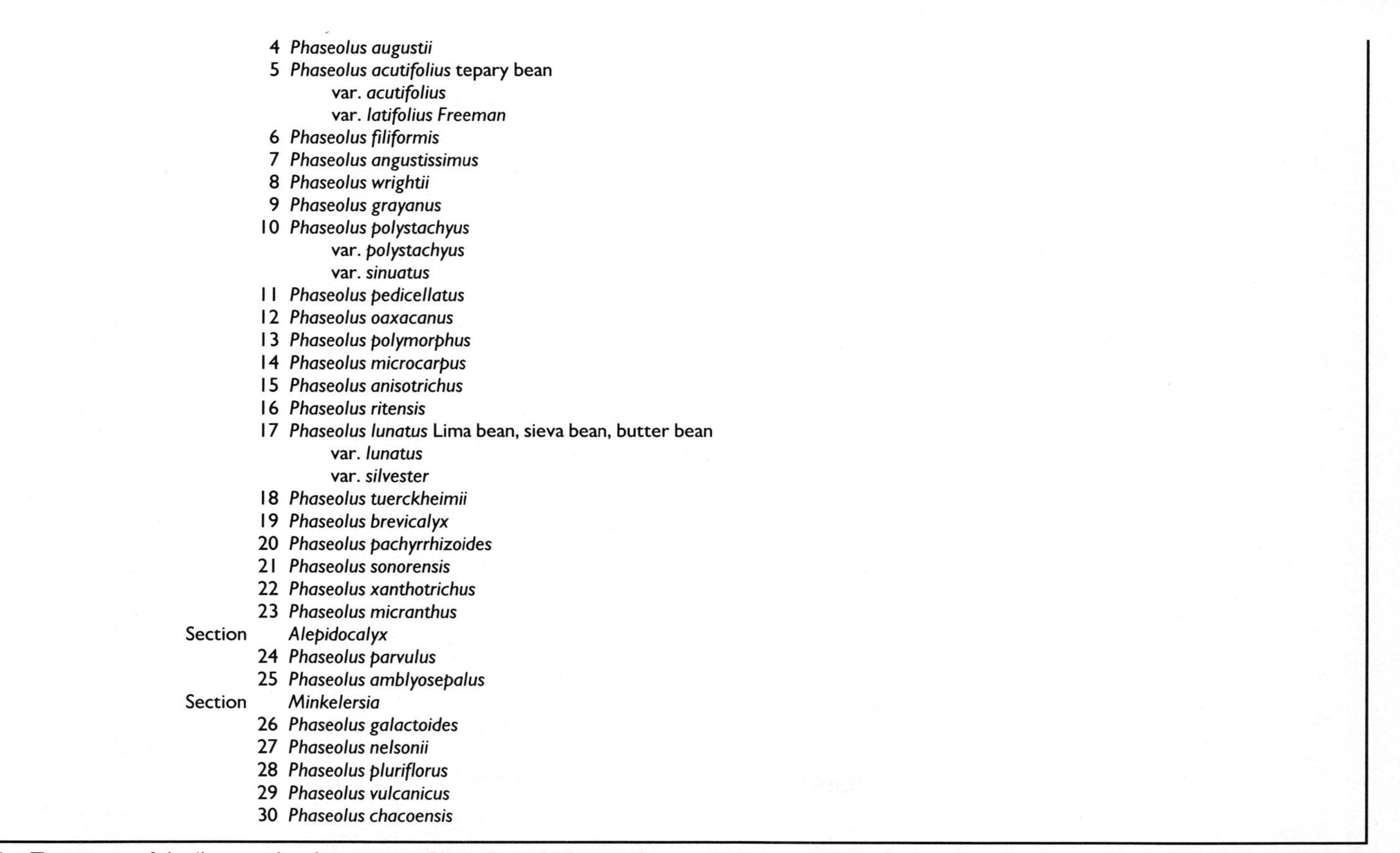

4 *Phaseolus augustii*
5 *Phaseolus acutifolius* tepary bean
var. *acutifolius*
var. *latifolius Freeman*
6 *Phaseolus filiformis*
7 *Phaseolus angustissimus*
8 *Phaseolus wrightii*
9 *Phaseolus grayanus*
10 *Phaseolus polystachyus*
var. *polystachyus*
var. *sinuatus*
11 *Phaseolus pedicellatus*
12 *Phaseolus oaxacanus*
13 *Phaseolus polymorphus*
14 *Phaseolus microcarpus*
15 *Phaseolus anisotrichus*
16 *Phaseolus ritensis*
17 *Phaseolus lunatus* Lima bean, sieva bean, butter bean
var. *lunatus*
var. *silvester*
18 *Phaseolus tuerckheimii*
19 *Phaseolus brevicalyx*
20 *Phaseolus pachyrrhizoides*
21 *Phaseolus sonorensis*
22 *Phaseolus xanthotrichus*
23 *Phaseolus micranthus*
Section *Alepidocalyx*
24 *Phaseolus parvulus*
25 *Phaseolus amblyosepalus*
Section *Minkelersia*
26 *Phaseolus galactoides*
27 *Phaseolus nelsonii*
28 *Phaseolus pluriflorus*
29 *Phaseolus vulcanicus*
30 *Phaseolus chacoensis*

Box 4.1 Taxonomy of the 'legumes' and one genus, *Phaseolus*, which provides us with 'common beans' – but there is more to beans than 'common beans' (from Smartt (1990) with kind permission of the author).

tremendous variety in this group which has yet to be studied in depth. In other words, amongst the legumes there are many species representing a rich source of genetic material but some are in danger of becoming extinct.

Ethnobotany and biodatabases

As well as species extinctions there are, of course, whole biological and human communities being destroyed, together with the vast stores of knowledge and experience of sustainable land-use built up by indigenous peoples over many centuries. For example, in the northwest Amazon basin over 2000 plant species are used as a basis for medicines by indigenous peoples. One single ethnic group was found to have knowledge of about 750 plant species which they believe to have medical properties. The combination of ethnobotanical studies (that is studies of indigenous peoples and how they use wild plants) with biodatabases has been one way of initiating the much-needed programmes for the protection of these indigenous peoples, their culture and their environment.

Tambopata Ethnobotanical Survey

During the last six years, students on expeditions and scientists from organizations throughout the world have been helping to create an important biodatabase about local people in Tambopata in Peru. All this is being done as a race against time because, like so many other indigenous peoples, their very existence is being threatened as a result of the destruction of the forests. The Institute of Economic Botany of the New York Botanic Gardens has been involved in this very important project. Logistic support for this work has come from the charity organization AMETRA 2001 (Aplicacion de Medicina Tradicional) which is based in Peru and was launched in 1987. One part of the Tambopata Project, during the latter half of 1985, was based on the Tambopata Wildlife Reserve in South East Peru, an area ethnically very rich. There, information about the uses and value (medical, cultural, spiritual, food, materials) of plants and animals together with general ecological information was recorded (table 4.1).

The primary motivation for the creation of the ethnobiological database in Tambopata was the conservation of the ecological and ethnic integrity of the Peruvian Amazon. Data emerging from this project serves as a stark reminder of the importance of conserving biodiversity. Without this work, we would be ignorant of the valuable properties of many plants. The only fear now is that knowing the importance of so many native plant species, these parts of the world may be exploited by the unscrupulous with no thought being given to the future health and safety of the indigenous peoples or their environment.

Table 4.1 *A summary of the uses of plants in Tambopata (Madre de Dios, Peru), as recorded in the Tambopata Data Base by Michel Alexiades. There is overlap between the number of species in each category.*

Use	*Number of plant species*
Materials	
construction (total – 53 plants)	
house building/furniture	43
thatching	8
boat building	4
others	4
fuel	15
tools, utensils and crafts	16
dyes, perfumes, gums and resins	10
fish poisons	3
others	4
	Total species 85
Food	
fruits	32
tubers	5
vegetables	3
seeds	4
spices and colourants	5
beverages	5
	Total species 42
Medicines	
gastrointestinal (total – 50 plants)	
diarrhoea	23
intestinal parasitosis	8
purgatives and laxatives	8
other	25
respiratory disorders (total – 28 plants)	
colds, coughs, flu	19
tuberculosis	11
circulatory system, including tonics and reconstituents	19
fever (total – 27 plants)	
malaria	6
others	21
Urogenital system (total – 46 plants)	
kidney disorders	14
venereal diseases	10
infertility and impotence	7
contraceptives	6
abortives	3
pre- and post-partum	7
others	4
skin (total – 33 plants)	
micosis	16
leishmaniosis	5
other	12
teeth (total – 16 plants)	
toothache	10
tooth decay (prevention/treatment)	9

Table 4.1 (cont.)

Use	Number of plant species
Medicines (cont.)	
eyes (total – 16 plants)	
conjunctivitis and infections	10
cataracts and loss of vision	6
blows, fractures, dislocations etc.	22
headaches	9
cuts, wounds and burns (total – 41 plants)	
homostats	10
antiseptics	18
circatrizants	17
painful joints	10
animal bites (snake, sting-ray, insect)	27
others	25
	Total species 153

4.2 The role of protected areas

Disappearing nature

Throughout the world, terrestrial native communities, such as forests, woodlands and heathlands, have progressively become smaller and the remaining areas have become more fragmented and isolated. This process, known as **insularization** has occurred throughout the world from temperate to tropical regions (fig 4.1). Insularization causes many changes amongst the wildlife. For example, as habitats become smaller some species will become extinct; so there is a reduction in the number of indigenous species which may then be followed by colonization by new invasive species. Thus the variety and composition of the species changes as the remaining habitats become smaller and smaller. All plant and animal species are dependent on other species for food and other resources and therefore the extinction of one species can lead to the extinction of another. There are some species upon which many others depend and these are called **keystone species**. For example, ants in tropical forests are keystone species, providing food for some predators and acting as pollinators for some plants. The extinction of the ants would therefore be disadvantageous for many other animals as well as plants.

One response to insularization has been to establish protected areas. These protected areas serve many functions, including the conservation of biodiversity, but they do have some limitations as nature reserves.

Types and functions of protected areas

There are many kinds of protected areas, ranging from national parks to nature reserves and all have different management objectives.

Some of the smallest nature reserves protect single trees or just one orchid, while large reserves, such as Ocean Sanctuary near Hawaii, afford protection to humpback whales (*Megaptera nodosa*). The legislation associated with protected areas is as varied as are the management objectives of protected areas (table 4.2) and some areas have several designations.

As well as areas especially designated for conservation, there are many other kinds of areas which provide relatively safe habitats for many plants and animals. These areas include roadside and railway verges, private gardens, cemeteries, hedges, some recreational areas, rivers, canals and ponds. In some countries there is a patchwork of habitats made up of varied manmade and natural habitats.

Selection of areas for nature conservation

In reality, economics and politics often dictate the selection of nature reserves but final selection should be always based on good scientific assessments. A major contribution to assessment of individual sites for nature conservation in Europe came in 1977 with the publication of *A Nature Conservation Review*. In that publication, Ratcliffe described and assessed ten criteria for evaluation of sites as a basis for the establishment of representative examples of natural areas. These criteria provide a useful basis for critical appraisal as well as a basis for conservation field studies. The following is a summary of the criteria (in no particular order).

1 *Size (extent)* This embodies the views that larger sites are better because they contain more species and that there is a minimum area which needs to be safeguarded in order to maintain the conservation interest of the locality.

2 *Diversity* This refers to both species and communities. However, although the general aim is to conserve areas rich in species and communities which are varied in structure, there are some interesting communities, such as heathlands, which intrinsically are plant species-poor and have a uniform structure.

3 *Naturalness* A rare condition in industrialized countries, but the types of habitats least modified by human activity should be given priority. However, some forms of traditional management, such as grazing of chalk grassland, is essential for the conservation of many chalk grassland species.

4 *Rarity* One of the most important purposes of a nature conservation area is to protect rare species. However, it is important to determine the factors which have made the species rare so that appropriate management of the species can be undertaken on the nature reserve.

5 *Fragility* This criterion reflects the degree of sensitivity of habitats, communities and species to environmental change and impacts caused by human activities. The most fragile ecosystems and species have high conservation priorities, but their conservation may be difficult and often requires large resources.

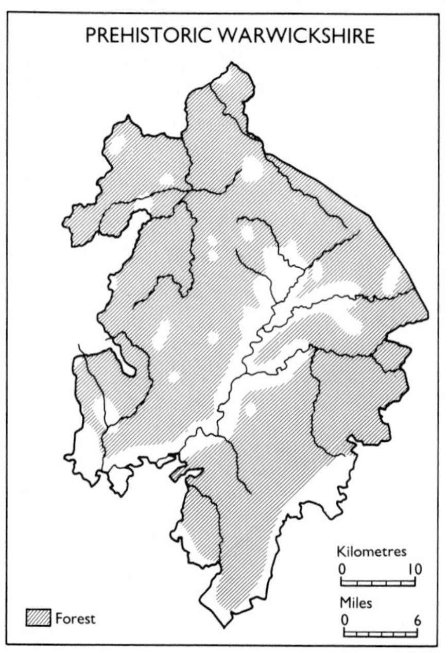
PREHISTORIC WARWICKSHIRE
Kilometres
0 10
Miles
0 6
Forest

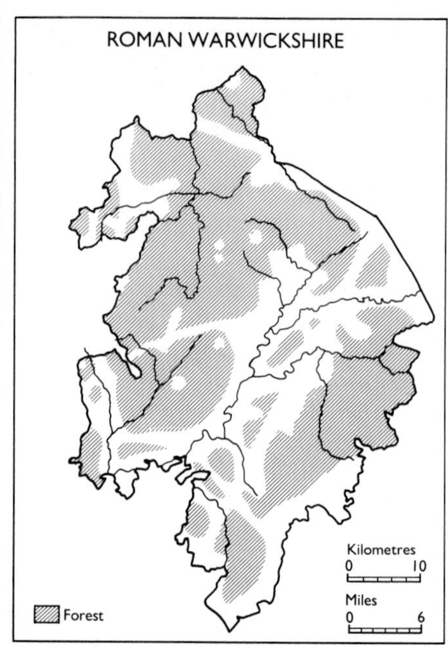
ROMAN WARWICKSHIRE
Kilometres
0 10
Miles
0 6
Forest

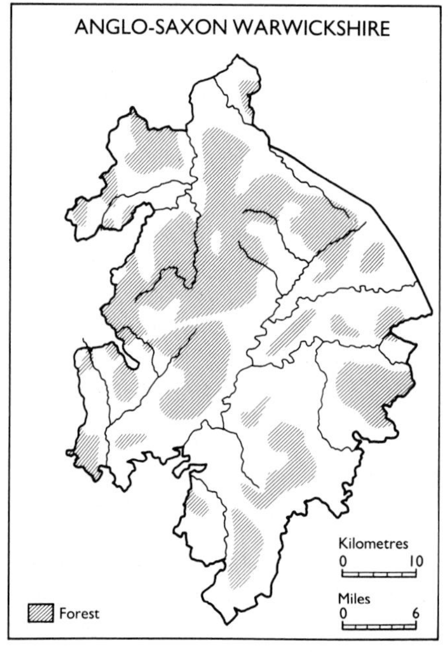
ANGLO-SAXON WARWICKSHIRE
Kilometres
0 10
Miles
0 6
Forest

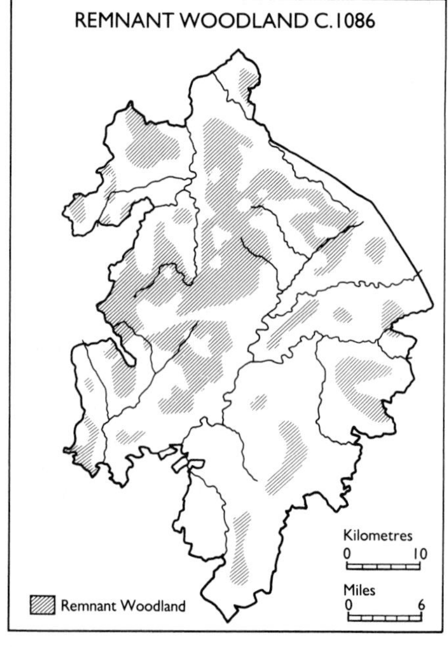
REMNANT WOODLAND C.1086
Kilometres
0 10
Miles
0 6
Remnant Woodland

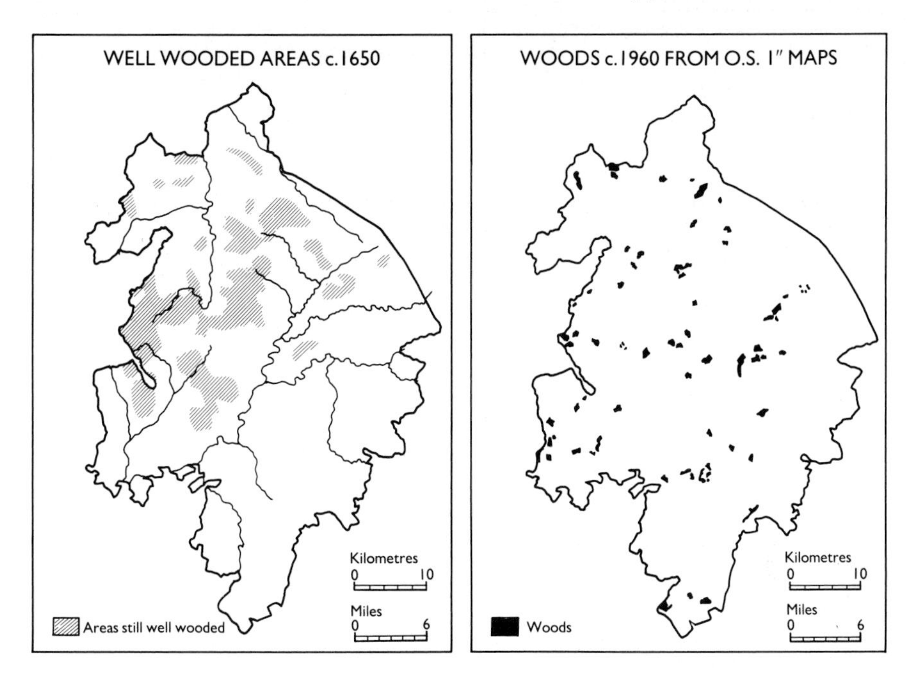

Fig 4.1 An example of insularization. This shows the decline and fragmentation of forests in Warwickshire, England from about 400 to about 1960 (from Thorpe 1978).

6 *Typicalness* The best examples of various communities or ecosystems should be selected, but their quality may be determined by features which are unusual. Unusual communities or ecosystems may have only a few available examples, whereas there may be a much wider choice of those which are typical or common.

7 *Recorded history* The extent to which a site has been used for scientific research is a factor of considerable importance. Long-standing scientific records enhance our understanding of conservation and may provide a basis for the analysis of ecological processes.

8 *Position in an ecological/geographical unit* Where practicable, and without lowering the standards of selection, it is desirable to include within a single geographical location as many as possible of the important and characteristic formations, communities and species of an area.

9 *Potential value* Sites which are of low current value, but which through appropriate management or even natural change show a potential for developing features of particular value in conservation, should be protected. This parameter is an amalgamation of other criteria and suggests that habitat creation is an important component of conservation (see p. 83).

10 *Intrinsic appeal* This is an interesting philosophical criterion. While

Table 4.2 *Protected Areas in Britain: nature conservation and landscape conservation.*

A Nature Conservation Areas	
Designation	*Statutory basis/control*
Biosphere Reserves	Countryside Commission, NCC.
Local Nature Reserves (LNR)	Local planning authority in consultation with NCC (National Parks and Access to Countryside Act, 1949).
Marine Nature Reserves (MNR)	Declared by the Secretary of State (Wildlife & Countryside Act, 1981).
National Nature Reserves (NNR)	Selected, designated and managed by NCC (1949 Act).
NGO Nature Reserves	Selected, designated and managed by non-governmental organizations: RSPB, County Naturalist's Trusts.
Private Nature Reserves	Non-statutory, developed by private individuals.
'Ramsar' Sites*	Wetland sites designated by Governments (Ramsar Convention on wetlands of international importance). NCC for Government.
Sites of Special Scientific Interest (SSSI)	Notified by NCC (1949 and 1981 Acts).
Special Protection Areas for birds	Member States of the EEC (Article 4 of the Council Directive on the Conservation of Wild Birds).
Biogenetic Reserves	Resolution (76) 17, Council of Europe, Committee Ministers. Not governed by a convention or directive.
B Protected areas which incorporate nature conservation	
World Heritage Sites	The 'World Heritage Convention', UNESCO, 1975.
Areas of Outstanding Natural Beauty (AONB)	Countryside Commission (1949 Act).
Country Parks	Non-statutory but designated by Countryside Commission in conjunction with local authorities and private bodies.
Environmentally Sensitive Areas	Designated by Ministry of Agriculture, Fish and Farming (Agriculture Act 1986).
Green Belts	Defined by local authorities within structure plans.
Heritage Coasts	Non-statutory and designated jointly by local authority and Countryside Commission.
MOD land	Some Ministry of Defence areas, by virtue of their restricted access, have become and are now managed as wildlife reserves.
National Parks (NP)	Delineated by the Countryside Commission and declared under 1949 Act.
National Scenic Areas	Scottish equivalent of NPs and AONBs.
National Trust land	National Trust Act of 1907.
Other areas or special areas	**1** Some areas (the Norfolk Broads, New Forest, Somerset Wetlands) have strict planning controls. **2** Roadside verges, recreational land, allotments, and many other 'green areas' are sometimes managed as nature reserves.

*See Lyster (1985) for details about international wildlife law and conventions.

science may view all organisms as equal, pragmatism dictates that in nature conservation it is inevitable that more weight will be given to some taxa than others; birds and colourful wild flowers arouse more enthusiasm than beetles or snakes. However, it is necessary that the conservation of less-popular groups is adequate.

Effectiveness of protected areas for biological conservation

Although about 4% of the world's land surface has been set aside for protection of plants and animals, and although there are now some marine nature reserves, most nature reserves are isolated and have not been located where there is a greatest need to conserve. Most nature reserves are designated in areas which serve no other purpose. Some have been established so as to save the last remaining fragments of a devastated landscape. For example, it has been suggested by many experts (WCED 1987) that 20% of tropical forest should be protected, but to date only 5% has been given any protection and some of that protection is inadequate because exploitation of the forest continues in various forms.

Most nature reserves, as remnants of what were once larger biotic communities, may result in the isolation of plant and animal populations and indeed may be too small to support all the resources required by them. Many nature reserves are surrounded by many kinds of land uses and this can lead to pollution and physical disturbance of the biotic communities on the reserve. Invasive species from the surrounding area may colonize nature reserves, for example large expanses of rhododendrons and bracken (*Pteridium aquilinum*) have created formidable problems on many nature reserves and national parks in England.

In general, larger reserves are better for conservation of biodiversity than small ones, but there can be no general rule because different nature reserves are established for different reasons. Nature reserves are very often surrounded by varied land-uses which prevents some plants and animals dispersing to similar habitats. However problems of isolation can be overcome, in part, by the establishment of wildlife corridors between nature reserves. One logical extension of this idea, supported in Western Australia, is a network of reserves interconnected by various kinds of corridors, such as lines of trees, scrub-covered banks or river edges. Buffer zones (see fig 4.6) around a nature reserve may help to reduce the effects of pollution and disturbance caused by activities in the area surrounding the reserve. One particularly interesting application of the use of buffer zones has been the zone established around Cameroon's Korup National Rain-forest Park which buffers the park against unfavourable disturbance but at the same time provides resources for 30 000 local farmers.

Who needs nature reserves?

The nature reserves of the world may have their limitations but nevertheless they have many valuable functions in addition to conservation. Natural history studies, educational studies and scientific research all benefit from wildlife on nature reserves. Nature reserves can help slow down the rate at which natural areas are damaged and can provide useful locations for long-term monitoring of changes in ecosystems. Some nature reserves are reservoirs of wild species which may provide genetic material for improvement of crop and grazing plants. Beneficial insects (such as predators of insect pests) and pollinators of fruit trees and other crop plants may depend on nature reserves for their existence. Above all, nature reserves and other kinds of protected areas provide enjoyment and are the last fragments of biotic communities in landsapes shaped and changed by humans. We all benefit from nature reserves and we need more of them.

4.3 Botanic gardens

Plants, as primary producers, underpin the rest of the living world. They provide food and habitats for consumer organisms, generate oxygen and play an essential role in soil formation and protection. Despite such importance, plants have a relatively low profile and are rarely the focus of conservation efforts. There is no plant equivalent of the giant panda or blue whale and yet if plant diversity declines so too does the diversity of all other life forms. Plants are ideally conserved in situ (where they occur naturally). In this way large numbers of individuals can be preserved with minimal management. Species are also able to continue evolving alongside their pollinators, symbionts and consumers. Native vegetation is offered a degree of safety within national parks and nature reserves, but habitat destruction outside these protected areas still leaves many species vulnerable. The International Union for the Conservation of Nature (IUCN) and World Wide Fund for Nature (WWF) estimate that, of the 250 000 species of higher plants, approximately 60 000 are in danger of extinction or genetic erosion in the next 30–40 years. The majority of these are to be found in the tropics where species numbers are highest. A potential solution to the threatened loss of diversity is conservation ex situ (off site). This is predominantly carried out in botanic gardens and arboreta (tree collections).

Botanic gardens were originally set up to cultivate medicinal species and later to house and display new plants which had been collected from abroad. They have unwittingly been engaged in plant conservation from their inception but since this was not their aim, a number of problems have been experienced. In the past botanic gardens have operated completely independently and their collections were acquired for their attractiveness or economic value. As a result some species have been widely collected while others are underrepresented. Acquisitions of new species often comprised of only a few individuals and little attention was paid to obtaining basic data about their source. In addition, there is an uneven distribution of botanic gardens and arboreta. There are approximately 1500 worldwide. Most of these are to be found in Europe, North America and USSR, whereas plant diversity is greatest in the tropics and subtropics.

In response to these problems a number of initiatives have been taken. At the forefront was the conservation of crop plants. Agriculturalists have long been aware that modern crops have limited genetic variation. In the 1960s the Food and Agricultural Organization of the United Nations (FAO) started a programme of genetic resource conservation. This has taken the form of a network of international agriculture research centres, each holding collections of germplasm for major crops. These centres are now coordinated by the Consultative Group for International Agricultural Research (CGIAR) which has its headquarters at the World Bank in New York. In 1974 CGIAR created the International Board for Plant Genetic Resources (IBPGR) with the aim of broadening the conservation of plant germplasm.

Three main methods are employed to conserve germplasm.

1 Field gene banks These are simply permanent living plant collections. They serve as a ready source of plants for research but they take up a lot of space and cannot include the full range of diversity that exists in the wild. In addition they are susceptible to pestilence and cannot be protected from natural disasters such as fire and flood.

2 Seed banks These represent a convenient and space-saving method of conserving germplasm. Some seeds can remain dormant for long periods if maintained at low humidity (<5%) and low temperature (− 20°C). Seeds that can be stored in this way are known as **orthodox**. These include many of the major crop plants, such as cereals, brassicas, carrots, beets, squashes, soybean, cotton, sunflowers, tomatoes and beans. A number of problems have yet to be solved, however. There is no non-destructive way of telling whether the seed is viable. It is therefore necessary to carry out regular germination tests; a time-consuming and costly exercise. Should viability fall below an accepted level the sample would need to be regenerated by growing plants which then produced new seed. This enforced inbreeding could lead to a loss of vigour (box 4.3). Some seeds are **recalcitrant**, that is they are damaged by drying and can only be stored for a few weeks or months. Examples include cocoa, coconut, mango, cinnamon, nutmeg, avocado and tea. Seed banks are also unsuitable for species which do not breed true, such as apples, species which depend on fungal symbionts, such as orchids, and species which normally reproduce vegetatively, such as potatoes.

3 Cryopreservation Cells from embryos and shoot tips can be used to generate new plants. Storage of these cells at very low temperatures (in liquid nitrogen at −196°C), in which all metabolic processes stop theoretically means that the material can be conserved indefinitely. In reality some cryopreserved tissue has proved to be chromosomally unstable over long periods.

The use of refrigeration for the preservation of plant material inevitably makes it susceptible to mechanical failure, but the major drawback of any of the three methods described is that the germplasm is also evolutionarily frozen. That is, it is no longer able to adapt and would soon become biologically obsolete, losing its value for reintroduction to the wild or for infusion into modern cultivars. The key to plant salvation is clearly an integration of conservation in situ and ex situ.

In 1989 the IUCN and WWF together with FAO, UNEP (United Nations Environment Programme), UNESCO (United Nations Educational, Scientific and Cultural Organization) and IBPGR produced the Botanic Gardens Conservation Strategy. This working document clearly outlines the action needed by botanic gardens to safeguard plant diversity (box 4.2).

The strategy also advises botanic gardens on how they can stop illegal trade in plant species. In 1988 a Convention on International Trade in Endangered Species (CITES) plant committee was established to monitor trade in plants and as a result now regulates import and export of all orchids, cacti, succulent euphorbs, *Cyclamen, Galanthus sternbergia*, most tree ferns and many carnivorous plants.

4.4 Zoos

Zoos have become an important refuge for many rare animals. At present it is thought that about 800 species of mammal, 800 species of birds and 400 species of reptiles and amphibians could disappear if there were no captive breeding.

Several species already owe their continued existence to the work of zoos. Two notable examples are Pere David's deer (*Elaphurus davidianus*) and Przewalski's horse (*Equus przewalski*). Pere David's deer was named after the French missionary who, in 1865, sent 18 specimens to zoos and parks in Europe. The deer subsequently became extinct in their native China but by 1981 the original 18 had given rise to a total captive population of 994. Similarly several specimens of Przewalski's horses, native of Mongolia, found their way into zoos of Europe, USA and Russia before they were hunted to extinction in the wild. By 1981 the total captive population had reached 425.

Conservation is a relatively recent aim of zoos. First and foremost, they were established as collections of animals for curiosity's sake. As such, zoos have not always placed the welfare of their captives too highly and as a result have not been universally appreciated. The sight of animals in cramped and sterile conditions, often engaged in disturbing repetitive behaviour, are anathema to animal lovers.

Thankfully now the tendency is to provide naturalistic surroundings, and the better zoos have made efforts to enrich the lives of their captives. The Zurich Zoo, for example has installed artificial termite mounds in the chimpanzee enclosure. These are loaded with sloppy foods such as yoghurt

The Strategy:

- *Recommends that each individual garden clarify its commitment to conservation in a Mission Statement and adopts more professional standards of management to achieve its Mission*
- *Provides the basis for a more coherent Accessions Policy that takes account of conservation needs and of what plants are held in other botanic gardens*
- *Outlines ways to improve the documentation of plant records and the verification of plant holdings, including computerisation to improve management of the collection and to facilitate exchange of data between institutions*
- *For* in situ *conservation, outlines the role of the garden in habitat evaluation, rare species monitoring, 'habitat gardening' and in managing protected areas*
- *For managed* ex situ *conservation, proposes strict rules and procedures for the establishment of seed banks, field genebanks and other germplasm collections, and outlines methods of sampling populations to maintain adequate genetic variation*
- *Emphasises the facilities which botanic gardens can bring to educating their estimated 150 million visitors each year*
- *Recommends that each garden provide a service to its local community as a resource and information centre*
- *Provides a framework for training of personnel, with emphasis on conservation.*

The Strategy is also concerned with how botanic gardens can best work with each other and with other organisations in achieving conservation. The Strategy outlines:

- *Who will participate in its operation*
- *Which are the priority regions where botanic gardens can best work with each other and with other organisations in achieving conservation*
- *Which are the priority species that most need conservation.*

It proposes that most emphasis be put on collaboration between gardens at the **national level**, or where appropriate, **regional level**. The Strategy proposes the structure for a national group and outlines a set of objectives.

The Strategy also recommends collaboration at the **international level**, through the IUCN Botanic Gardens Conservation Secretariat, though this should be less formal and less structured. The Strategy outlines a programme of 'North–South' technical liaison between botanic gardens and calls for a global programme of monitoring and coordination of cultivated collections.

Box 4.2 The Botanic Gardens Conservation Strategy (from WWF & IUCN, 1989).

and porridge which can be obtained by inserting twigs in the same way that a wild chimp would get termites. Such efforts have increased the breeding success of some inmates, often a sign of good health.

In a conservation context the aim of captive breeding is to preserve the genetic stocks of threatened species so that they can be reintroduced to the wild when conditions permit. Zoos, though, tend to have only a few individuals of each species and, unless there is close cooperation with other zoos, lines would soon become inbred and seriously weakened as a result (box 4.3). Consequently breeding programmes need to be carefully controlled. To this end the International Species Inventory System (ISIS) was set up at Minnesota Zoo to advise which individuals to exchange for breeding; a sort of animal dating agency. It would seem to be a fairly expensive business, ferrying would-be suitors around the world, not to say traumatic for those involved. Nevertheless this is preferable to keeping all of the breeding animals in one place. The technique of artificial insemination, commonly used in farming, is one solution. Frozen sperm can easily be distributed and has the added advantage that it sidesteps quarantine regulations. On the farm, sperm is collected by getting a bull to mount a dummy cow and catching the ejaculate in a giant condom. Such a procedure is only possible because the bull is reasonably docile. Collection of sperm from an elephant or a lion poses a trickier, not to say more dangerous, proposition. Thankfully, from the keeper's point of view, sperm can be collected from an anaesthetized animal using a probe which electrically stimulates the genitals. This method could also be used to obtain fresh supplies of genes from the wild without further depleting stocks.

The reproductive potential of animals can be increased by embryo transfer. This practice involves obtaining eggs from a captive female who has been induced by drugs to superovulate. These are then fertilized in a test tube and the resulting embryos transferred into a surrogate mother of a closely related species. This technique has been successfully carried out at the Bronx Zoo, New York, where a gaur calf (*Bos gaurus*), a wild cow from India and SE Asia, was born to a Holstein milk cow mother (*Bos taurus*).

The success of captive breeding has ironically created the problem of overproduction. There are two solutions to this problem, birth control and culling. Stopping reproduction though may destabilize a family group. Continuity is important for some animals, such as the primates, which learn about motherhood from direct observation and as individuals age their fertility may drop. The alternative often invokes some objections on ethical grounds. However, it should be appreciated that in the wild mortality is high and not many animals make it to old age; only 20% of lion cubs, for example, reach adulthood. Life expectancy is therefore much less than can be achieved in captivity. Wild lions rarely live beyond seven years whereas 20 is commonly reached in zoos. In the absence of natural checks populations of captive animals would soon exceed the zoos' carrying capacity. Consequently euthanasia has become an inevitable and essential part of zoo management.

Reintroduction of animals to the wild has so far met with limited success. The Arabian Oryx (*Oryx leucoryx*) is one exception. This animal was virtually hunted to extinction but saved by a breeding effort which began in 1962. By 1979 a total captive population of 322 had been achieved, and in 1982, 14 were returned to Oman. Their future looks promising.

Efforts to reintroduce the Hawaiian goose (*Branta sandvicensis*) have so far proved difficult. In 1949 the wild population was reduced to about 12

Within a population there exists a number of harmful, recessive alleles. These are normally masked in the heterozygous state. Inbreeding (breeding between closely related individuals), however, increases homozygosity and some of the harmful recessives are expressed. This leads to a decrease in fitness. Medical records of the Dorcas gazelle (*Gazella dorcas*) at the National Zoo in Washington have shown that inbred calves are twice as likely to perish in the perinatal period than outbred calves and also are more vulnerable during the first six months.

To overcome this problem scientists need to determine the minimum viable population (MVP). The MVP is dependent on two factors:

1. How much diversity must be preserved? During each act of reproduction only half of the alleles are passed onto the next generation. As a result some diversity may be lost; the more generations the greater the loss. It has been estimated that for most animals a breeding population of about 500 individuals is needed to maintain genetic diversity.
2. How much initial diversity? As a general rule, the smaller the founder population the larger the MVP needed to maintain diversity. For most species, though, a founder population of 20–30 is enough. More important is how quickly the founder population can grow to the MVP; the more offspring produced per generation the less diversity will be lost. This may explain the relative success of Przewalski's horse and Pere David's deer breeding programmes from small founding populations.

Box 4.3 Inbreeding.

birds but captive breeding at the Slimbridge Wildfowl Trust in Gloucestershire and other places around the world have ensured its survival. 3000 birds have been released back into the wild but it still has not managed to re-establish a viable population. The major problem with reintroductions is that the conditions that caused the animal to become endangered in the first place have remained unchanged. In the case of the Hawaiian goose the introduced predators are still there.

Despite these problems it is essential that animals are reintroduced to the wild as quickly as possible. Captive breeding will inevitably lead to the artificial selection of such characteristics as docility. In addition, learned behaviour such as finding food, establishing territories and wariness of humans would soon be lost. Primates, in particular, depend on their parents showing them which of the vast array of food types available are edible and which are poisonous. As with plants, the long-term future of endangered animals clearly lies in the integration of conservation in situ and ex situ.

Conservation is also served by zoos in the areas of research and education. Zoos represent a practical and valuable stage for the study of wild animals. In fact London Zoo which was opened in 1828 was established to promote the study of zoology. There, for example, regular veterinary attention has revealed a great deal about animal physiology. Data from blood samples from the mammals, birds and reptiles which had been treated over the last 16 years have been gathered together in a data bank called Lynx. Such data forms an important source of information for the management of captive animals and treatment of wild ones.

Zoos are ideally placed to educate the general public. In 1982 it was estimated that the 757 zoos of the world attracted 357 million visitors. Information about individual species alongside name plaques is provided to stimulate the interest of the visitor. Some zoos arrange their animals in taxonomic groups to illustrate evolutionary relationships while others may arrange them geographically to highlight their origins. Brookfield Zoo in Chicago has attempted to create the illusion of a tropical rainforest in an enormous indoor exhibit. In these naturalistic surroundings a community of rain forest animals are housed giving the visitors a 'total experience' of this threatened environment, one that they are unlikely to gain first-hand. Such an experience helps people relate to what is being lost when rain forests are being destroyed.

4.5 Conservation of species endangered by trade

Illegal trade in wildlife and their products threaten many species with extinction. In response to this threat the 1972 UN Conference on the Human Environment created CITES, the Convention on International Trade in Endangered Species, as part of the United Nations Environment Programme (UNEP). The convention came into force in 1975 and by August 1990 had attracted 109 signatories (member states). The implementation of the convention is coordinated by a secretariat which has its headquarters in Lausanne, Switzerland. It is funded by contributions from the member states and is charged with the control of the international trade in wildlife and their products. It does not seek to stop trade completely but rather to encourage it in a sustainable way. Sustainable utilization of living resources is seen as a legitimate practice (see 1980 IUCN World Conservation Strategy, box 2.1) which has the potential for generating valuable income for developing countries, typically the major exporters.

CITES is enacted by a system of three appendices which correspond to the status of species in relation to trade (box 4.4). Each member state is required to create two bodies to operate the convention. Firstly a national Management Authority which is responsible for issuing certificates and export permits and secondly a national Scientific Authority to advise the Management Authority. The convention is enforced by customs officers. The member state is also required to submit trade records to CITES. These are incorporated into computerized data bases at the World Conservation Monitoring Centre at Cambridge and analysed to support management decisions.

The CITES constitution requires that meetings are held every two years. This gives the opportunity for appendices to be updated.

The basis for assembling and updating appendices comes from the data that are available. In some cases this is barely sufficient. Therefore, the

Appendix I: Species threatened with extinction which are or may be affected by trade

No commercial trade of these species is permitted, but certificates of exemption and export permits may be issued under restricted circumstances, such as for specimens bred in captivity or artificially propagated, or for scientific research. Among those species listed are:

all apes	Asian elephant	some parrots
all lemurs	African elephant	some crocodiles
Giant panda	Cheetah	Coelacanth
Great whales	Leopard	some shells
all rhinos	Tiger	some orchids and cacti

Appendix II: Species which may become threatened with extinction unless trade in specimens is subject to strict regulation

Commercial trade is closely controlled by the issue of export permits and some restrictions may operate such as marking of products and imposition of export quotas. Among those species listed are:

all primates*	some antelopes	some corals
all cetaceans*	all crocodiles*	medicinal leech
all hummingbirds	all owls	all cacti*
all pythons*	all sea turtles*	all orchids*

* except species already listed in appendix I

Appendix III: Species requiring protection in certain states only

Export from listed countries requires a permit whereas export from other countries needs a certificate of origin.
Among those species listed are:

Common hippopotamus (Ghana)
Cuvier's gazelle (Tunisia)
Royal cobra (India)

Box 4.4 CITES appendices.

secretariat is also charged with the task of organizing appropriate studies and finding external funding (table 4.3).

CITES has achieved a great deal in the 15 years since its inception. The high number of parties to the convention would seem to indicate global concern over the problem of unregulated trade and a willingness to cooperate. There are still a number of problem areas, however. Finance, as usual, is in short supply and many proposed external projects remain unfunded. Moreover the use of trader's money to fund external projects has aroused some criticism. It even led to some claims that the $200 000 that the ivory traders had given towards the CITES ivory unit had biased the lobbying of the secretariat against a total ban at the 1989 meeting.

Huge profits encourage many to circumvent the convention. Poaching is still widespread, documents are forged and large consignments are still intercepted by customs officers. Some parties, namely Egypt, Ecuador, Italy, Senegal, Spain and Thailand were reluctant to pass on trade records

Table 4.3 *Some examples of CITES projects in progress in 1991.*

Project	*Cost ($)*	*Main contributors*
Ivory unit	425 000	EEC, USA, UK, JGMIA, WWF, ivory traders
Caiman in South America	190 000	EEC, JP, USA, WWF, caiman traders
Status and trade of green turtles	180 000	JP, JGMIA
Status of the Nile crocodile	125 000	EEC, JP, Switzerland
Plant identification manual	20 000	JP

Acronyms: EEC, Commission of the European Communities
JP, Government of Japan
JGMIA, Japan General Merchandise Importers Association
WWF, World Wide Fund for Nature
Source: CITES Doc. 0042Z 1990

hinting perhaps that the convention was not being strictly adhered to. In addition, it is inevitable, that with so many signatories that disputes would arise. The option of lodging a reservation, whereby signatories can free themselves from amendments to the convention is an inescapable element of international treaties; without this option aggrieved members would simply leave. The problems of regulating trade in an endangered species can be clearly illustrated by the case of our largest land animal, the African elephant (*Loxodonta africana*) (fig 4.2).

The African elephant – endangered by the trade in ivory

In the last ten years African elephant numbers are reported to have declined from about 1.3 million to 625 000, largely as a result of the ivory trade. In 1985 the CITES ivory unit was set up to coordinate a system of ivory export quotas. The system required that ivory exported from member countries be accompanied by a special permit and unworked ivory stamped with a country code, a unique serial number, year of marking and the weight. The governments of producer countries were called on to implement the controls and new members to CITES were given an amnesty on existing stockpiles.

The high value of ivory and weak internal security of producer countries undermined the initiative and elephants continued to disappear at the rate of 100 000 per year. In 1988 it was estimated that over 80% of the ivory leaving Africa was illegal. In addition elephant populations were becoming seriously distorted with respect to sex and age. The older males yielded the greatest weight of ivory and were therefore the first to be taken. A recent survey of elephants in Amboseli National Park in Kenya showed that males only accounted for 22% of the population, and in Tanzania's Mikumi reserve a mere 0.4% were male. The average age of herds also fell, forcing the poachers to hunt smaller animals. The average tusk weight dropped from 9.8 kg in 1979 to 4.7 kg in 1987. Consequently more animals were needed to maintain supply.

Fig 4.2 A herd of African elephants in Amboseli National Park, Kenya (credit M. Boulton/ICCE).

Elephant populations in some countries dropped dramatically. In Kenya, for example, the population dropped from 130 000 in 1973 to just 16 000 in 1989. In Uganda the population dropped from 18 000 to 1900 in the same period. The situation had become so critical that in 1989 some countries, Tanzania, Kenya, Gambia and Somalia, proposed that the African elephant be transferred to appendix I to ban all further commercial trade. In response to the crisis the USA and EC, who between them accounted for about 64% of the world's consumption of ivory, unilaterally banned imports. The proposal was passed and came into force in January 1990 but was not universally supported. Seven member countries posted reservations, namely Botswana, China, Malawi, South Africa, UK, Zambia and Zimbabwe. (The UK reservation was entered on behalf of Hong Kong for a period of six months to permit disposal of legally held stocks.)

The African nations that posted reservations argued that while the elephant numbers in some countries had dropped, theirs, through good management, had increased. Between 1979 and 1989 for example, numbers had risen from 30 000 to 43 000 in Zimbabwe, 20 000 to 51 000 in Botswana and from 7800 to 8200 in South Africa. In Zimbabwe such management involved the transfer of game ownership from the state to the land owners. As a result elephants were looked upon as a valuable resource. A single animal could generate $3500 for ivory, meat and hide and possibly $1500 as a trophy fee. The Zimbabwe Wildlife Department earns $3 million per year by culling. Such profits provide cash for development projects and therefore encourage sustainable culling and make poaching antisocial.

The debate continues to rage. The pro-ivory producers claim that numbers have been massaged by sentimental westerners to create a panic in the name of elephant conservation. The reality, they argue, is that if elephants had no monetary value there would be no incentive to tolerate crop damage and the animal would be destroyed as a pest. They would also cite the case of the black rhino which has continued to decline despite an appendix I listing.

The anti-ivory lobby argue that it is only through legal trade that illegally obtained ivory can find an outlet. They would also suggest that as elephant numbers continue to fall poachers will eventually turn their attention on the herds of the pro-ivory countries. In fact there is already some evidence that poachers are crossing the border from Mozambique to plunder ivory from the Gona-re-Zhou game reserve in Zimbabwe.

4.6 Marine conservation

The seas and oceans make up approximately two-thirds of the Earth's surface. They represent an enormous environment, but their inhabitants have not escaped pollution and overexploitation. Marine conservation is therefore primarily concerned with addressing these two problems.

Pollution

So vast are the open seas that they would seem difficult to defile. The coastal zone, the shallow strip between the land and the edge of the continental shelf, on the other hand, is far more vulnerable. It has become a dumping ground for sewage, heavy metals, pesticides, hydrocarbons and radionuclides. One possible consequence of this abuse is the increased frequency of algal blooms. The algae release toxins which are fatal to many marine organisms, and when the bloom dies it becomes a substrate for bacteria which deoxygenate the water.

Some pollutants are directly toxic while others may lead to reduced fertility or suppressed immunity. The death of 16 000 seals in the North Sea epidemic of phocine distemper virus during 1988/9 was thought to be due, in part, to reduced resistance caused by high levels of PCBs (polychlorinated biphenyls). The exact way in which pollutants affect marine organisms remains a mystery in many cases. The death of 250 bottle-nosed dolphins off the east coast of the USA in 1987 was thought to be due to pollution but no link was firmly established.

Much of the pollution is fed into the coastal zone by rivers. The rivers which enter the North Sea for example annually discharge 500 000 tonnes of nitrogen, 46 tonnes of phosphorus, 110 tonnes of mercury, 1100 tonnes of cadmium, 21 800 tonnes of lead and 107 100 tonnes of zinc. The solution to this damaging human activity would seem straightforward. Controls on discharges, however, are expensive and some countries are reluctant to make the necessary investment, especially when many of the links between pollutant and deaths of marine organisms are not established. The actions of environmental groups such as Greenpeace and Friends of the Earth have stimulated some response but progress has been slow.

Overexploitation

Overexploitation of marine organisms is a perennial problem and has led to the serious depletion of many species. Several important fisheries have collapsed as a result, such as the Alaskan salmon industry which at its peak in 1936 was producing 180 000 tonnes per year. The decline of whales is described below.

As stocks of one species decline hunters systematically harvest new ones depleting each in turn. This is evident in the North Sea at present where the decline in white fish has promoted fishermen to expand their sand eel fishery. Sand eels are a dietary component of white fish and sea birds such as guillemots and puffins. Their subsequent decline, therefore, has already seriously affected the breeding success of these birds and may also hinder the recovery in numbers of white fish.

The overexploitation of marine organisms is also due in part to advances in technology and to the international nature of the seas. Beyond the

Table 4.4 *Great whales* (Source: L. Watson *Whales of the World* (Hutchinson 1985)).

Whale	*Status*	*Whale*	*Status*
Great right	2 000	Blue	9 000*
Bowhead	3 000	Minke	700 000
Pygmy right	unknown	Sei	80 000
Grey	15 000	Bryde's	20 000
Great sperm whale	500 000	Humpback	5 000
		Fin	4 000

*Some scientists estimate the status of the blue whale to be only about 1000.

economic exclusion zones of coastal states, now set at 200 miles by the Third UN Conference on the Law of the Sea, the water is known as the high seas and open to all. Regulation of hunting in these waters relies on conventions but, as we shall see, these are only effective if ratified by all member states.

The history of whaling is a classic example of overexploitation on the high seas. The whales which have been commercially hunted are predominantly the baleen whales together with the great sperm whale (table 4.4). Their numbers have been severely reduced to the extent that some species, particularly the blue whale, may not recover.

Whales yield large quantities of useful products and therefore have been relentlessly pursued. A single blue whale, for example may contain 110 barrels of oil (1 barrel = 36 gallons). The invention of the harpoon gun and the deployment of factory ships hastened the depletion and by 1946, the year that the International Whaling Commission (IWC) was established, bowhead, grey and right whales had already been hunted to commercial extinction. In the following 20 years populations of blue, humpback, fin and sei whales had been similarly reduced.

The conservation of whales is controlled mainly by The International Convention for the Regulation of Whaling which is regulated by the IWC (box 4.5). First attempts to conserve whale stocks by the IWC clearly failed. The Commission was able to make recommendations but had no means of enforcement. Amendments to the Convention required a three-quarters majority (excluding abstentions) and were binding to all parties although members had the option of objecting within 90 days thereby freeing themselves of the change. Moreover, a member country is free to leave the commission whenever they choose. Consequently the IWC was effectively powerless to control the self-interest of member states. Great profits were to be made and there was little incentive for restraint. It was not until pressure from non-whaling nations came to bear, that some action was taken. The 1972 UN conference on the Human Environment was a turning point in this respect. In 1946 the membership of the IWC was made up of whalers, but as stocks fell some nations, such as Britain, Australia, Canada, New Zealand, South Africa, Netherlands and the USA

900: First records of commercial whaling
1868: Invention of the harpoon gun
1924: First factory ship
1932: Association of Whaling Companies drew up an agreement to limit production in the interests of market stability.
1946: International Convention for the Regulation of Whaling. The International Whaling Commission (IWC) is established with the aim of safeguarding whale stocks for the purposes of whaling.
1972: UN Conference on the Human Environment calls for a 10-year moratorium on commercial whaling. Rejected by IWC: 4 for, 6 against and 4 abstentions.
1973: IWC propose commercial moratorium: 8 for, 5 against and 1 abstention, but rejected because ¾ majority needed for decision.
1980: IUCN, UNEP and WWF produce World Conservation Strategy which calls for a moratorium on commercial whaling.
1982: IWC declares moratorium: 25 for, 7 against and 5 abstentions, but delayed until 1986 and to be reviewed in 1990. Japan, Norway, USSR and Peru object (Peru subsequently withdrew objection).
1986: Iceland and South Korea engage in scientific whaling.
1988: Japan and Norway stop commercial whaling and engage in scientific whaling.
1990: Japan, Norway and Iceland propose limited resumption of minke whaling – rejected.

Box 4.5 The history of whaling.

dropped out of whaling and joined the call for a moratorium (a temporary halt to assess the status of whales). Such a proposal was initially defeated by the three-quarters majority clause, but by 1982 enough non-whaling nations had been recruited to swing the vote. Not surprisingly the most ardent whalers, such as Japan, Norway and the USSR, objected and continued to hunt (fig 4.3). Commercial hunting finally stopped in 1988 but Japan, Norway, Iceland and South Korea still take whales for scientific purposes. A proposal to resume limited hunting of minkes was defeated at the 1990 annual meeting of the IWC but the whalers remain determined.

The moratorium was declared because not enough was known about the numbers of whales to be able to determine sustainable yields (catches that do not jeopardize future stocks). The calculation of these yields requires values for gains and losses which in turn are derived from population data on age structure, age of sexual maturity, rate of reproduction and life expectancy.

The physical difficulty of studying organisms in the vastness of the open ocean means that such data are difficult to obtain. The only sure way to obtain a satisfactory census is by identifying individuals and following their movements. Some success has been achieved with the right whales, by virtue of their conspicuous callosities (bristle patches) and humpback whales with their tail flukes. These apart, estimates are almost entirely dependent on data from the whaling industry. This has led some whaling nations to continue whaling 'scientifically' in order to collect the data necessary to satisfy the IWC.

Fig 4.3 Minke whales alongside a Russian whaling vessel in the south Polar Seas (credit Lady Phillipa Scott/ICCE).

The question now posed is 'Should the moratorium on whaling ever be lifted?' The anti-whalers claim that whales are highly intelligent creatures that suffer greatly in the manner that they are caught and killed, whereas the whalers argue that whales are a legitimate resource, which are no different to pigs or chickens, that can be sustainably harvested once stocks have recovered.

Coral reefs

Coral reefs are highly productive ecosystems found mostly in shallow tropical waters. Their biological richness rivals that of the tropical rainforests. A single reef may contain 3000 species. They are extremely long-lived but very vulnerable to adverse human activity. Heavy silting, perhaps from soil erosion, can be a rapid cause of coral mortality. An increase in nutrients can preferentially favour growth of algae leading to the deterioration of coral. Reefs are also threatened by the ravages of collectors who supply the aquarium trade and souvenir industry.

Unlike tropical rainforests, however, the coral reefs are unlikely to suffer extinctions. This is because they do not house large numbers of endemic species and the majority of organisms have a free-swimming larval stage which means they can disperse over great distances. In fact, when a community is destroyed, its locality may be recolonized by different organisms to the ones that were initially present. This does not mean of course, that they should be abused. As well as harbouring a diverse array of wildlife, coral reefs also provide a valuable source of income through tourism. In 1986 the estimated total income from Australia's Great Barrier Reef was just over A$100 million.

Marine reserves

There are a number of differences between marine reserves and terrestrial reserves. Firstly the problems facing marine environments tend to have their origins on land, whereas the major threat to terrestrial environments is habitat destruction. Terrestrial reserves are generally accessible to the public while the underwater world is only visible to a few snorklers and scuba divers. Finally, marine ecosystems tend to require less management than land-based ones. Consequently, marine reserves are a relatively recent phenomenon and fewer in number. In fact it was not until the 1981 Wildlife and Countryside Act that marine reserves were established below the low-water mark in Britain. Coral reefs reserves have been in existence for longer; by 1980 there were about 40 worldwide.

Given the nature of the marine environment it may be pertinent to question the value of protected areas. Such activities as mining and dredging can be prohibited, but if experience on land is anything to go by this may not be very effective. In temperate regions cold water and limited visibility would mean very few visitors and the major threat would come from onshore pollution. In addition, the survival of migratory fish could not be assured by protection of small areas. Consequently efforts might be better invested in tackling the pressing problems of pollution and overexploitation.

Marine reserves may be more worthwhile in tropical waters. They could ensure that activities were controlled in such a way that the impact of tourists was minimized. The licensing of users could generate income which in turn could be used to further protect the region. A system of zoning is employed within the Great Barrier Reef. Some zones are for the exclusive use of research, some for education, some for recreation and some for general use. Such a system could easily be adapted for the management of other reef reserves.

4.7 Wetlands conservation

Biology and ecology of wetlands

Wetlands are temporarily or permanently waterlogged areas bordering aquatic ecosystems. They include estuaries, wet peatlands, marshes, mires, fens, swamps, floodplains, deltas, coastal lakes and lagoons. Some wetlands, such as swamps and mires, may appear quite unattractive yet they can support a rich biodiversity and provide data in the form of preserved pollen deposits and other biological deposits from which we can learn a lot about past environments. Whereas some wetland ecosystems, especially waterlogged examples, are the least productive, others are the most productive of all ecosystems.

Estuaries and other coastal ecosystems, such as mangrove swamps, experience a wide range of physical and chemical conditions. Salinity, temperature and oxygen levels vary widely in these areas and this variation, coupled with water and sediment movements, culminates in a complex and wide range of environmental conditions which provides conditions for high levels of productivity (that is the rate at which biomass is produced by green plants). Estuaries, along with marshes and swamps, are amongst the most productive ecosystems in the world and such high levels of productivity supports a rich variety of animal life, especially wading birds. Mangrove swamps and reed beds are valuable wildlife habitats, but they are severely threatened the world over.

Degradation and losses of wetlands

Of all ecosystems, wetlands have suffered the greatest losses and damage as a result of human settlement and also as a result of changes in land use. More recently, ever-increasing demands on water resources and global changes in climate pose a great threat to the world's wetlands. In Saudi Arabia, for example, extraction of ground water for agriculture has caused a lowering of the water table. Such intensive use in arid regions can never be sustainable. Even in temperate countries, such as Britain, the lowering of water tables, caused partly by too much water abstraction, is becoming commonplace with disastrous consequences. In the USSR, overexploitation of the rivers for irrigation of cotton crops has resulted in a greatly reduced Aral Sea (Aral'skoye More), an area of water that was once the fourth largest lake in the world. The disappearing Aral Sea and the excessive use of agrochemicals on vast monocultures of rice and cotton has resulted in a major environmental disaster and a human tragedy. As yet little publicity seems to have been given to the implications of the loss of the Aral Sea.

Throughout history, there has been a tendency for humans to settle in and around estuaries. This has happened partly because estuaries on the one hand are near a source of fresh water and on the other hand they provide a rich source of fish and other marine life for food. In low-lying areas, some coastal wetlands act as natural flood barriers and prevent rising flood water from reaching inhabited areas: the economic value can be immense (see p. 88). Other wetlands are used for dumping of treated sewage and thus act as a tertiary waste treatment site. Unfortunately, human impact on estuaries and other coastal areas, such as salt marshes, has resulted in losses of these areas and pollution of many of those that remain. In some parts of the world, the sediments in estuaries have become so badly polluted with persistent chemicals and heavy metals that such areas will remain polluted for many decades, even if the source of pollution were removed today.

Many other wetland areas have been subject to exploitation or so-called reclamation (that is they are drained prior to a change in land use). The peatlands of Europe are under threat as never before because of the extraction of peat for fuel and for horticultural purposes. This exploitation results in loss of biodiversity as well as the loss of unique habitats. Also, funds coming mainly from the Common Agricultural Fund are being used to reclaim marshes and estuaries for recreation, fish farms and airports throughout Europe.

For many years, there have been losses of wetland areas which were not only valuable in terms of wildlife but also in terms of their importance to agriculture. Many flood plains throughout the world, rich as they are in fertile soils, are dependent on regular flooding in order to maintain fertility. These floods have occurred regularly since ancient times but impacts on watersheds and water catchments have had dramatic effects on water movement patterns (Anderson & Grove 1987). Trees and other vegetation hold back water so that there is a steady flow to the rivers. Deforestation removes that steady flow resulting in unpredictable flooding, that is flooding which occurs too quickly or no flooding at all.

Conservation of wetlands

After many years of draining, reclaiming and adapting wetlands for agriculture and urban development, some countries have come to realise that there is a need for strong legislation to protect these areas. The USA, in particular, has enacted several Federal laws for the protection of their wetlands. Landmarks in the international recognition of the importance of wetlands have been the Ramsar Convention (see p. 17) and the IUCN Wetland Programme which was approved in 1985. The Ramsar Convention has prompted a wide range of initiatives, including the establishment of protected wetlands, and the IUCN Programme, with a global network of experts, has initiated a strong scientific basis for management and conservation (box 4.6).

As well as protecting and managing wetlands for wildlife, there is a need to use these ecosystems in a wise and sustainable manner (something which is embodied in the Ramsar Convention). The critical wetlands in Africa have, for example, recently been the focus of contracting parties to the Ramsar Convention and in 1989 11 African countries had signed the convention and designated 30 wetlands (fig 4.4). In 1989 the Ugandan Ministry of Environmental Protection established a national Wetland Conservation and Management Programme. This has developed out of the Government's concern with the growing rate of loss and damage to wetlands and a growing awareness of the importance of wetland ecosystems for people and wildlife. One of the aims of the Programme is to

The IUCN Wetlands Programme coordinates and reinforces activities of the Union concerned with the management of wetland ecosystems. The Programme focuses upon the conservation of ecological and hydrological processes, in particular by developing, testing, and promoting, means of sustainable utilisation of wetlands. It does so in collaboration with IUCN members and partners, in particular those other international institutions with a specific wetland mandate, especially the Ramsar Convention Bureau, and the International Waterfowl and Wetlands Research Bureau (IWRB).

Mangroves in North Sulawesi, Indonesia. Credit: WWF/M. Dépraz

Box 4.6 The IUCN Wetland Programme (from the *IUCN Bulletin*, **20**, April/June, 1989).

develop a national policy for conservation and the sustainable use of wetlands. To achieve this it will be necessary, in the first place, to establish an inventory of the wetlands and then undertake a detailed assessment of the functions and values of the wetland ecosystems.

4.8 Conservation of tropical rainforests

Destruction of tropical rainforest is probably seen as the major current threat to biological diversity. The rainforests are confined to areas of high rainfall and high temperature, and are found in a broad equatorial belt between 30°N and 30°S (fig 4.5). They cover just 7% of the land surface but are home to at least 50% of all living species. The reasons for such diversity are discussed in box 4.7. In addition, a great number of these species are endemic, not only to their respective land mass but also to their forest type. Recent studies by Erwin on beetles have shown that very few species are widespread (table 4.5).

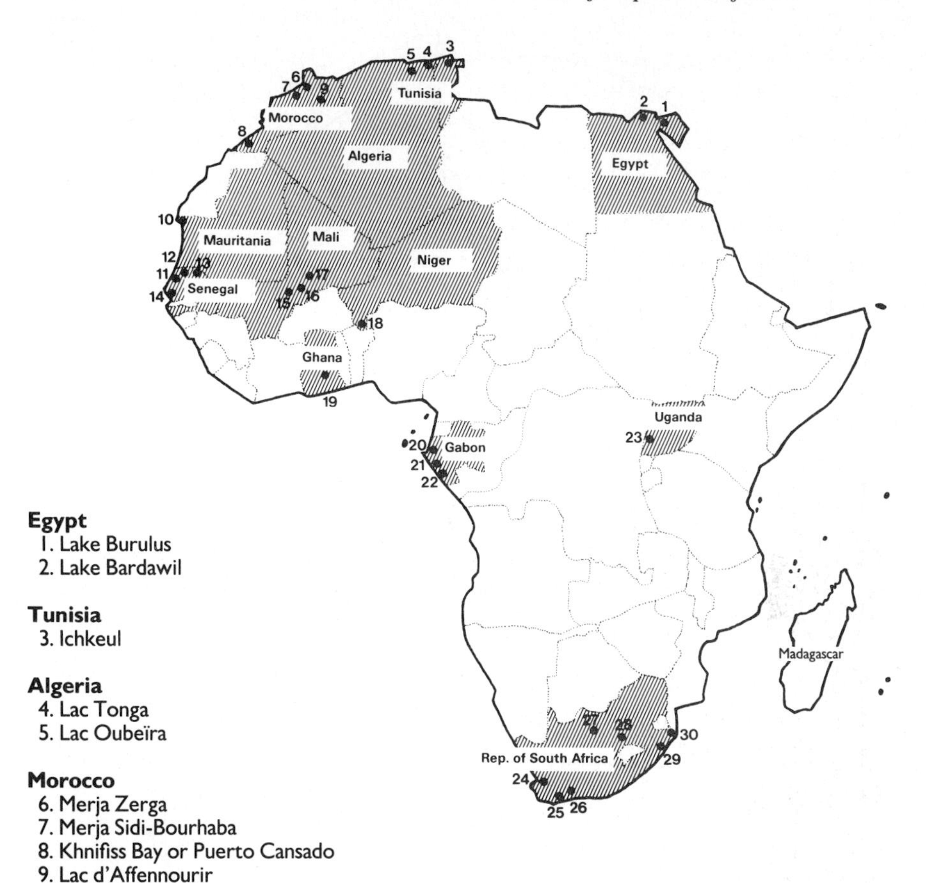

Egypt
1. Lake Burulus
2. Lake Bardawil

Tunisia
3. Ichkeul

Algeria
4. Lac Tonga
5. Lac Oubeïra

Morocco
6. Merja Zerga
7. Merja Sidi-Bourhaba
8. Khnifiss Bay or Puerto Cansado
9. Lac d'Affennourir

Mauritania
10. Banc d'Arguin

Senegal
11. Réserve spéciale de faune de Gueumbeul
12. Parc national des Oiseaux du Djoudj
13. Bassin de la Réserve spéciale de faune du N'diaël
14. Delta du Saloum

Mali
15. Séri
16. Walado Debo/Lac Debo
17. Lac Horo

Niger
18. Parc national de "W"

Ghana
19. Owabi Wildlife Sanctuary

Gabon
20. Réserve nationale de Wongha-Wongha
21. Parc national du Petit Loango
22. Réserve de Setté Cama

Uganda
23. Lake George

South Africa
24. Langebaan National Park
25. De Mond State Forest
26. De Hoop Viei
27. Barberspan
28. Blesbokspruit
29. St Lucia System
30. Turtle Beaches/Coral Reefs of Tongaland

Fig 4.4 Ramsar Convention sites in Africa (from *The Quarterly Newsletter of the Convention on Wetlands of International Importance Especially as Waterfowl Habitats*, April 1989).

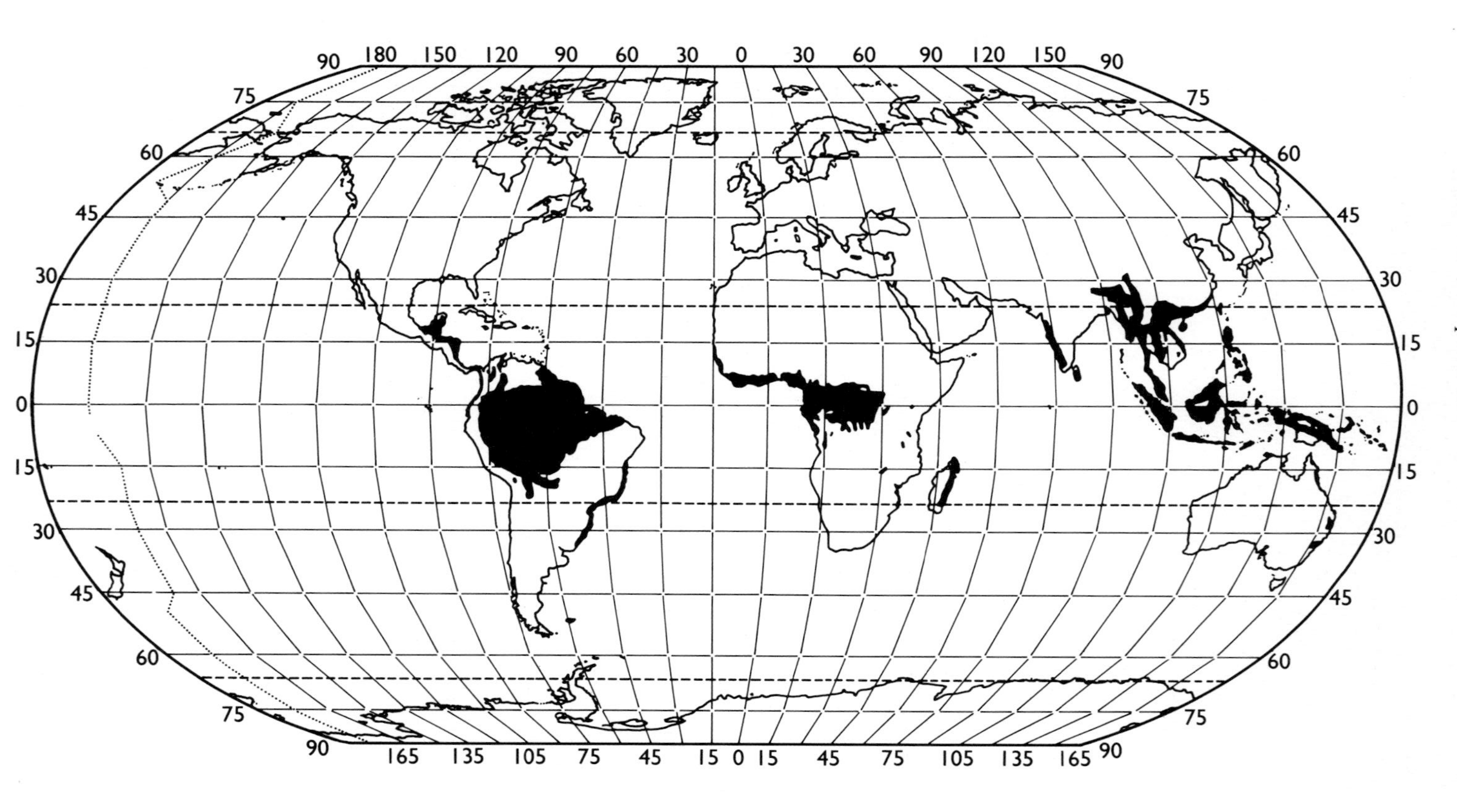

Fig 4.5 Tropical rainforests (from N. Myers, *The Primary Source: Tropical Forests and Our Future*, New York, W.W. Norton, 1985).

Table 4.5 *Endemism in tropical rainforests (from T.L. Erwin. The tropical forest canopy, the heart of biotic diversity, in* Biodiversity, *ed. E.O. Wilson (1988)).*

Site	*Manaus (Brazil)*	*Tambopata (Peru)*	*Manaus/Tambopata*
regime	4 forest types	upland forest type I 2 plots	upland forest type I
	>70 km apart	50 m apart	1500 km apart
number of species	1080	126	113
shared species	1%	8.7%	2.6%

The reasons for the diversity are complex and not fully understood, but several hypotheses have been suggested. To begin with high temperatures and high rainfall provide ideal conditions for photosynthesis and make tropical forests among the most productive of ecosystems.

Ideal conditions normally seem to favour domination by a few aggressive species which leads to low diversity. This apparent paradox can be explained in a number of ways. Firstly, the forests, rather than being homogeneous are actually made up of a patchwork of habitats. These range from evergreen moist forests through deciduous forests to mangrove swamps. Secondly, tropical forests are among the oldest terrestrial ecosystems. They have been unaffected by the ice ages that have struck temperate zones, and as a result every possible niche has been filled. Although not subject to catastrophic change tropical forests have experienced climatic shifts. This has created island effects within the forest providing optimum conditions for speciation. High rates of herbivory keep plant numbers at sub-competition levels. (Normally two species are not able to share the same niche because one species will always outcompete the other; the **competitive exclusion principle.**) As a result there is a high degree of niche overlap, that is species are able to exploit similar niches and therefore there are more species per unit area. High productivity and high diversity of plants provide a wide range of non-uniform habitats which in turn gives rise to high animal diversity.

Box 4.7 Why are tropical rainforests so biologically diverse?

Current rates of deforestation threaten to completely clear the world's tropical rainforests within 120 years, probably sooner because of population pressure (see section 3.1). It is inevitable that some species have already been lost and many more are at risk. Rainforests are a fragile ecosystem. Once deforested, soil erosion and change in microclimate seriously limit its ability to regenerate. There are several causes of rainforest destruction.

Shifting agriculture. This is a primitive form of agriculture in which the forest is cleared to grow crops. The forest vegetation is then burnt to release its nutrients, but these are soon exhausted and after two or three years the process must be repeated in another part of the forest. This was traditionally carried out at a low level, which allowed regeneration, and did little harm to the forest. A growing rural population and an uneven distribution of land, however, have increased the pressure on the forest. In tropical Latin America, for example, just 7% of the land owners possess over 90% of the arable land. As a result the landless peasants are forced into the forest, intensifying shifting agriculture and reducing the prospect of the forest re-establishing itself.

Cattle ranching. This is the major cause of rainforest destruction in Latin America. It is partly driven by an increasing world demand for beef, but is also related to cultural factors. Cattle raising is associated with social standing and political power. As a result beef production expanded rapidly with a large proportion destined for foreign markets. Costa Rica, for example, increased its cattle herd from 900 000 in 1960 to 2.2 million in 1980, while local consumption of beef dropped by 40%. Pastureland is established at the expense of forest and, as with shifting agriculture, results in the loss of soil fertility. Consequently the land is abandoned and more forest is destroyed.

Logging. The tropical timber trade is largely centred in South East Asia. Indonesia, Malaysia and the Philippines account for over half of all hardwood exports. In 1980 this was worth $2.2 billion to Indonesia and was second only to the oil in terms of foreign revenue. Despite, or perhaps because of, the value of this resource, trees are mostly cut at an unsustainable rate and often in a destructive and wasteful way. The selective removal of valuable species invariably results in the loss of surrounding trees. Surveys in SE Asia have revealed that logging irreparably damages between one-third and two-thirds of residual trees.

Industrialization. Mining and dams for hydroelectric power contribute greatly to forest destruction. The flooding of the Tucurui dam in the north-east of Brazil led to the loss of 2430 sq km of forest.

The high levels of diversity and fragility of this ecosystem mean that conservation must be aimed at maintaining the standing forest. This could be achieved in two main ways. Firstly by setting aside forests as protected areas and prohibiting further destructive human activity. To date 5% of tropical forests have been designated as protected areas. It would be unrealistic, though, to imagine that the whole ecosytem could be conserved in this way. The forests must accommodate a growing population and are seen as a valuable resource by the developing countries which own them.

The second alternative is to promote sustainable utilization or non-destructive use of the forest. Land ownership patterns clearly need to be reformed and permanent and sustainable agriculture encouraged. High rainfall and poor soils make conventional farming inappropriate in the forest. There would seem to be no reason, though, why the ideal conditions for plant growth cannot be harnessed to grow crops more suited to the region. Plantations would protect the soil and watershed but monocultures invariably attract pestilence. An alternative would be to grow a range of crops, including legumes to enrich the soil nitrogen, as carried out by traditional forest farmers. The Hanunoo people of the Philippines, for example, grow about 40 crops to the hectare while the Lacandon people of Mexico manage up to 80 species per hectare. By utilizing a range of crops at different levels the farmer is imitating the natural diversity of the forest and gaining its inherent advantages. Ironically the very people who possess the knowledge to farm in this way are themselves threatened by the destructive nature of unsustainable practices.

Sustainable forestry is a subject of debate at present. Trade in tropical timber is thought to be worth about $8 billion per year and a valuable source of income to the countries which own rainforest, but stocks have tended to be destroyed rather than managed. In 1984 the International Tropical Timber Organization (ITTO) was established to encourage sustainable utilization, conservation of rainforests and maintenance of their ecological processes, roughly in line with the aims of the World Conservation Strategy. The organization is supported by 36 producer countries and 33 consumer countries, but little progress has been made so far. It has been estimated that less than 1% of forests are managed sustainably.

Some argue that commercial pressures, heavy machinery, and corruption make sustainable management impossible and that the only way to save forest is to exclude commercial loggers. Others claim that the forest can only survive if it has economic value and point to the example of the Philippine Islands of Mindoro and Marinduque, where deforestation increased following the banning of logging. In order to achieve the ITTO objectives, though, it is generally agreed that a number of conditions need to be met. Firstly, logging needs to take place in selected areas and carefully controlled to minimize damage to the forest. In addition, tropical timber must be profitable. At present most wood is exported as logs whereas the greatest profit is to be gained from processed timber.

Among the alternative uses of standing forest, tourism appears to be limited at present. Forests are dominated by plants and insects which tend to have low appeal. The few larger mammals that they do contain, such as the orang utan and tiger, are difficult to trace (unlike the lions and elephants of the African savannah which are on open view). The sheer diversity of lifeforms, though, may prove an attraction in the longer term.

Perhaps the best option may be to exploit the natural diversity of the intact forest. The list of non-timber products that can be obtained from the forest is virtually endless. They include vegetables, fruits, nuts, spices, tannins, oils, rubber, waxes, drugs and many others. What is more, it has been calculated that non-timber products are more valuable than the timber itself. The major advantage of standing forest is that it can be harvested year after year whereas pasture for cattle raising has a limited lifetime and timber extraction is effectively a one-off operation. And, of course, the forests are conserved.

4.9 Conservation in the urban environment

The urban environment

The buildings, impervious surfaces and various forms of pollution in cities and towns can have far-reaching environmental effects, including climatic effects. For example, heat is generated by many activities in urban environments. This leads on average to an increase in temperature, despite losses in sunlight caused by high buildings and losses in insolation (solar heat) caused by dust and carbon dioxide accumulation in the atmosphere. There is accumulation of metals in plants and movements of heavy metal through the urban ecosystem; there is the direct chemical effect of toxic gases on the vegetation; there are changes in species composition and there are the direct effects of noise and lights on some fauna, especially birds.

Although it is well known that urbanization results in losses of wildlife and habitats and that there are interactions between the built environment and wildlife, there has been little monitoring of the cumulative effects of wildlife and habitat losses in any city. Local authorities have information on rates of expansion of the built environment but there remains the opportunity for someone to look at the cumulative effects of losses of green areas (parks to back garden) in built-up environments.

Effects on plant and animal populations

Although some more tolerant, ubiquitous species (such as starlings, *Sturnis vulgaris* and plantains, *Plantago major*) survive well in urban environments, and although some species such as the European red fox (*Vulpes vulpes*) readily adapt to the urban environment, urbanization results in loss of habitats and therefore a net loss in species. Indeed, there are some startling examples of losses of wildlife in urban environments: for example less than 2% of the Atlantic forests within the urban area of San Paulo in Brazil remain and through this destruction it has been estimated that thousands of species (some endemic and many not described) have become extinct.

Within cities there is a decrease in the number of natural or semi-natural habitats as you move toward the inner built-up areas and many forms of wildlife are affected. For example, the interesting effects of this pattern of distribution of 'green areas' on bird populations has been well studied in London (Cousins 1982). A map of London was divided into squares (based on the national grid), each square being 10 × 10 km. Records of breeding species were collected for each square and then aggregated to presence or absence of breeding species in each of the 24 10 × 10 km squares covering the whole of London. In the case of land birds, Cousins found that, in addition to a decline in species density with increasing urbanization, there is a decline in the size of bird species towards central London: larger species are not present in the central areas.

Value of urban wildlife

The benefits of wildlife in urban environments are many. It is known for example that vegetation may be an important 'sink' for heavy metals. In Budapest, for example, it has been shown that the leaves of some tree species accumulate heavy metals and, as well as being used as an indicator of pollution, the leaves help to remove the metals during the clearing of the autumn litter. Parks and other wooded areas in the urban environment can be important in helping to reduce the extremes of the urban climate. Indeed, in larger industrial cities it is thought that stretches of wooded areas radiating out from the cities to the countryside (airways or green corridors) with unimpeded flow of air could help to reduce temperature extremes and improve air quality by removing dust and airborne chemicals. It seems therefore, that trees and other plants have many functions in an urban environment such as dust filters, wind breaks, sun-shades, assimilators of carbon dioxide and producers of oxygen. Urban parks and gardens have an important function as a place to relax and simply enjoy the natural world. Some would say that urban 'green areas' even have a therapeutic value, a value easily appreciated when so many people seem subjected to stressful life-styles.

The populations of some urban species can serve as useful indicators of changes in the environment. Lichens, for example, because of their sensitivity to air-borne pollution, have been used as sentinel indicators of pollution. These indicator species can also be used to monitor the effects of any attempts to reduce pollution levels, for example, in larger industrial cities, few pollution-tolerant lichens are found near sources of pollution. The further the distance away from the pollution, the more sensitive species will survive and thus the greater the variety of lichen species. In instances where sources of pollution have been removed, there has been a gradual increase in the number of lichen species.

Biological conservation in the urban environment

There is much research being done on conservation of wildlife in the urban environment, much of which has been aimed at single species (such as foxes or raccoons) or groups of species (lichens, birds). These research programmes throughout the world have made some very important contributions to urban conservation (box 4.8). Broadly speaking, there are two main approaches to conservation in urban areas: one using improved and protected 'green' areas and the other by way of habitat renewal and restoration.

A simple survey of an urban area will reveal that there are many wildlife habitats to be found among the buildings, between roads and alongside

NATURE CONSERVANCY COUNCIL

Urban wildlife news & MaB

Vol 7 No 2 May 1990

NCC's Urban Programme 1990/91

The Community Nature Scheme is the most exciting developme… in the NCC's Urban Programme in1990/91 … this aside, the NCC is not putting apprecia… …r staff time into this area of work tha… …litan cou… Englanc… enthus… help r…

The … pro… str… C… F…

… in the … nentatio… Although … elp here, o… some loca…

authorities to coordinate work. As … carry out a strategy we … authorities to identify … Local Nature Reserve…

Very important among… wildlife in towns is the … from it. The use of natur… …lso seen to b… …o encourage … …eople about th… …eir area so th… …edge and increased. Th… NCC helps in this …tional level with our publications. We are … involve people … in inner cities and … estates. We a… …o give a … National C… to help de… …ities.

Ecosystems studies in Argentina

Work is being carried out in Argentina to try to integrate the development of San Miguel de Tucumán, the agricultural areas nearby and the Biological Park of Sierra de San Javier, which rises above the city. Research involves natural, productive, and urban ecosystems. The work is being done partly by the Universidad Nacional de Tucumán and partly by the Fundación Ibatín and makes an interesting study of the environment and human settlements. An environmental strategy for the San Miguel de Tucumán/Sierra de San Javier ecosytems has been produced by the university (*Estrategias para el Ordenamiento Ambiental del Ecosistema Gran San Miguel de Tucumán - Sierra de San Javier*). This short document describes the characteristics and functioning of the natural and the urban ecosystems and outlines environmental strategies. The people working in this programme would be interested to hear from others working in similar fields.

For details contact Arq. Julio César Corral, Universidad Nacional de Tucumán, Parque Biológico Sierra de San Javier, Jujuy 457-4000 San Miguel de Tucumán, Republic of Argentina

New urban wetland in Utah

A flood control wetland recently constructed in Salt Lake County, Utah, has become home to spotted sandpipers, belted kingfishers, and black-headed grosbeaks among many others. The landscaping plan was proposed by the Utah State Non-game Biologists who worked with the developers, contractors and public agencies to implement the scheme with the volunteer help of local junior high school students in planting and seeding the area. The good wetland habitat created has given local people in the surrounding residential area the enjoyment of close contact with the plants and animals which are establishing themselves here. The National Institute for Urban Wildlife has applauded the people of Salt Lake County for putting into practice the approaches to integrating storm water control with nature conservation which the Institute has long advocated. Their booklet *Urban wetlands for stormwater control and wildlife enhancement* by L W Adams and LE Dove (1984) is well worth looking at and details can be obtained from the Institute at 10921 Trotting Ridge Way, Columbia, Maryland 21044, USA

Urban studies in Asia

Hong Kong and Lae (Papua New Guinea) provided the focus for two of the early-starting pilot projects within the Man and Biosphere Programme concerned with ecological approaches to the study, management and planning of urban systems. Subsequent studies included those on suburban Bangkok in Thailand, Gwachon New Town and Seoul in the Republic of Korea, and Kuala Lumpur and the contiguous Klang Valley in Malaysia. The experience and findings of these projects provided the backcloth to a small regional workshop on tropical urban ecosystem studies, which took place at the Universiti Kebangsaan Malaysia (National University) in Bangi, Malaysia, from 18-21 January 1988.

Urban Green Project in Kuala Lumpur

An exciting new Urban Green Project has begun in Kuala Lumpur in Malaysia. It is sponsored by the Institute of Advanced Studies of the University of Malaya under the direction of Lim Teck Ghee, Professor of Malaysian Land Studies. The field surveying and mapping is being co-ordinated by Dr Jack Rieley of the University of Nottingham, England

Roundabout wildlife in Shepherds Bush

A traffic roundabout in West London may seem an unlikely site to attract the attention of a wildlife organisation. However, the London Wildlife Trust, with financial aid from British Gas, spent a November Sunday planting the Shepherds Bush roundabout, at the junction of the M41 and Holland Road, with shrubs including berberis, hawthorn and guelder rose. These will look nice and help wildlife too. The Trust hopes that the project will appeal to local people as well as to drivers using the road.

People's enjoyment of wildlife is important (Photo: The Guardian)

Informal international meeting in Berlin

Early June saw five members of the NCC's Urban Habitat Network join in Berlin with representatives of the London Ecology Unit, Moscow State University and the University of Lund to study the very advanced programmes of research, planning and land management in West Berlin

Box 4.8 Conservation projects for the urban environment (extracts from the *NCC Urban Wildlife News*).

factories. However, the gardens, roadside verges, amenity areas, riparian habitats (edges of streams and rivers), allotments and other areas are but small fragments of what were much larger habitats.

It is difficult for some species of plants and animals to travel across the built environment and so, therefore, some populations become isolated. One way to overcome this problem is to establish ecological corridors or wildlife stepping stones. Hedges, streams and rivers and even roadside verges, if managed correctly, can, in theory, help facilitate movements of animals and plants between fragments of habitats in urban areas. Some cities have combined recreational and conservation objectives with the result that wildlife corridors in the form of linear habitat fragments can function as greenways; the result being that humans and wildlife benefit.

Management of parks and recreational areas can dramatically improve the species-richness of both plants and animals and restore some of the losses in natural biodiversity. The widespread use of exotic plants in parks and gardens needs to be considered very carefully, particularly as appropriate varieties of native species can be of equal aesthetic value but can also contribute to the restoration of natural ecosystems.

Urban grasslands are all too often managed as manicured and ecologically 'sterile grass deserts'. Many of these grasslands could be made more attractive, at no more cost (or even reduced cost) in terms of time, labour and energy, if there was enrichment with native grass and herb species. One simple but valuable method of parkland grass management is to mow some areas less frequently than others and others not at all (see p. 100). Less-frequent mowing can result in an increased richness of plant species within a year or so.

Despite all the efforts to conserve wildlife in urban areas, there is an ever-increasing pressure on remaining fragments of woodlands, grasslands and aquatic habitats. However, because of the growing concern for losses of wildlife and the growing enjoyment of wildlife, there have been efforts to incorporate buffer zones between developments and natural habitats (fig 4.6). The aim is to establish an area of land which acts as a buffer against physical disturbance and pollutants. For example, pressures on a woodland in the vicinity of a new housing development could be relieved if an amenity area of grassland and shrubs were kept between the houses and the woodland. Without an amenity area or buffer zone, the edges and later the inner parts of the woodland would soon be damaged as a result of trampling, build-up of litter and colonization by plants common to urban gardens but not natives of woodland.

4.10 Biological conservation and agriculture

Developments in agriculture

It is not surprising to learn that agriculture is the most common land use throughout the world. In the last five decades there has been a

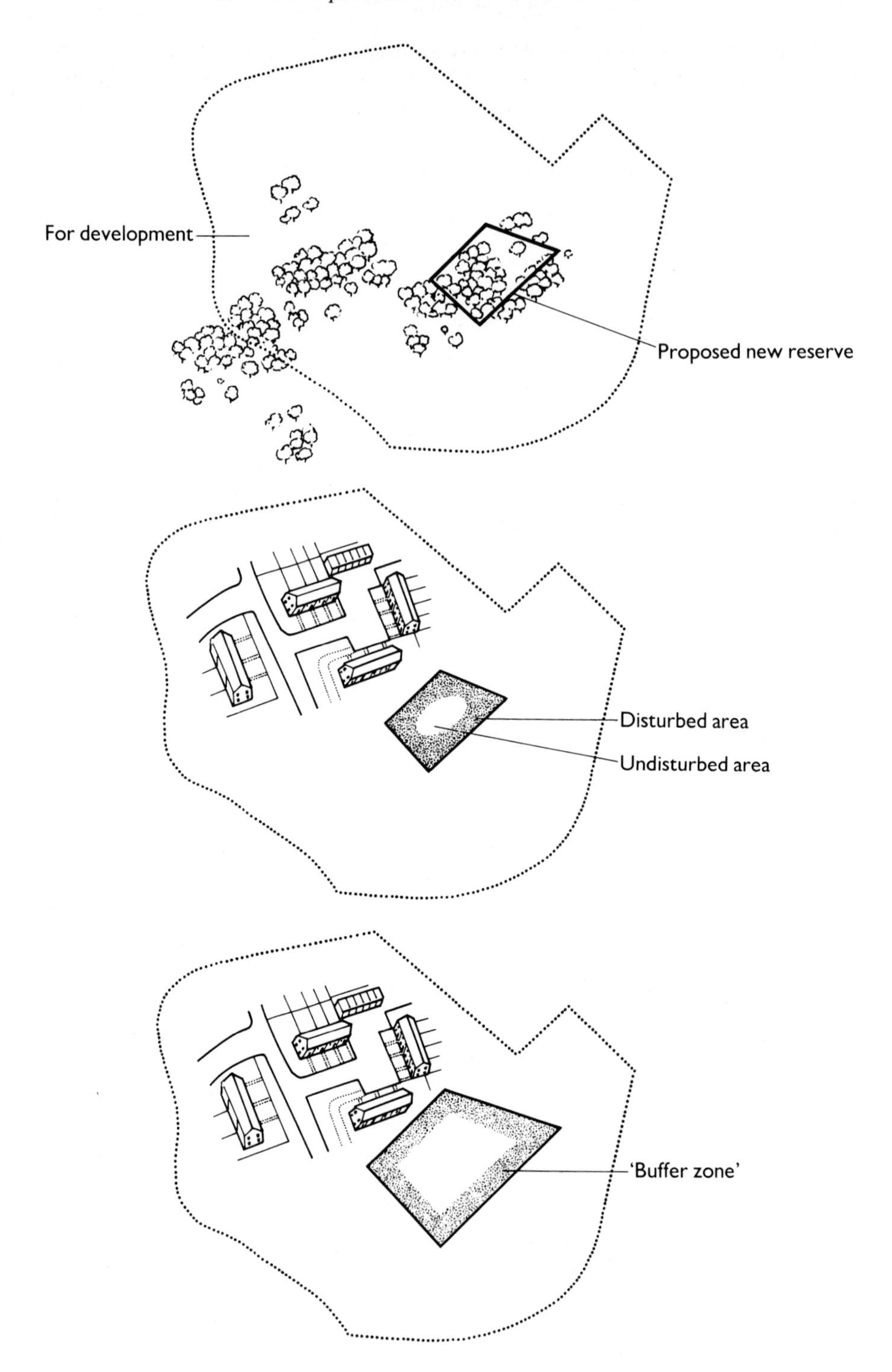

Fig 4.6 The buffer zone concept for conservation of urban woodlands.

tremendous development in new agricultural techniques and at the same time a very large increase in land being converted to agriculture. Agricultural productivity has been greatly increased to try and meet the increasing demand for food.

Increased productivity can be attributed mainly to the following:

1 development of new, genetically uniform varieties of plants which are resistant to disease and attack by insects and other organisms;
2 use of artificial fertilizers;
3 increased use of pesticides, fungicides and other agrochemicals;
4 more use of irrigation;
5 development of agricultural machinery for large-scale and rapid processing of crops.

Such developments were the basis for what was called the 'green revolution', which commenced in the 1920s and 1930s with increased yields in temperate regions, then later in the tropics and subtropics. For many years it was never doubted that the 'green revolution' would solve the world's food problems, and indeed there have been very great advances in food production. New plant varieties continue to be developed and genetic engineering may play an increasingly important role in increasing food production. However increased population growth means that there are more hungry people in the world than ever before.

Modern agriculture: the environmental costs

No one would dispute the tremendous benefits brought to us by modern agricultural practices but there are costs to human life and to the environment. Some of those costs are now so serious and long-lasting that we need to assess whether or not some agricultural practices should be changed, perhaps with decreased productivity. For the same reason we may need to reconsider whether or not agriculture in some areas is really the most useful form of land use.

In many parts of the world there have been considerable political and economic pressures to bring more and more land into agricultural production. However, in some areas intensive agricultural techniques have resulted in damage to soil structure with the result that prime agricultural land is being lost to erosion and desertification. At present rates, close to a third of the world's arable lands may no longer be suitable for growing crops within 20 years and for every 1.2 million hectares lost we lose the ability to provide food for a million people (ICCE 1984).

Large areas of land with monocultures provide ideal conditions for the build-up of high population densities of pests. Control of these pests by use of agricultural chemicals has resulted in increased crop yields and thus helped to feed millions of people. At the same time the extensive use of chemicals has resulted in severe problems. One study quoted by the World Commission on Environment and Development (WCED 1987) reported that approximately 10 000 people die each year in developing countries from pesticide poisoning. Commercial fisheries, wild birds and harmless insects have been greatly affected by the intensive use of pesticides.

Despite the effectiveness of agrochemicals in killing pests, some of those pests become resistant to the chemicals and there seems to be a never-ending spiral of development of new chemicals and increase in resistant species. Over 400 species of pests are now resistant to at least one pesticide and the proportion of crops in the USA lost to insects has approximately doubled since the 1940s, to reach 13%, despite the fact that the use of pesticides has increased. But what is perhaps most worrying about the use of agricultural chemicals is the fact that there are very few studies which look at the long-term effects of agrochemicals in ecosystems and very few studies which monitor long-term effects on non-target organisms.

Agriculture, conservation and sustainable development

Modern agriculture is not always in conflict with biological conservation. Along with advances in modern agriculture there have been some most encouraging developments that not only conserve nature but also contribute to a more cost-effective agriculture.

Many organizations have been responsible for promoting ways to manage living natural resources which permit sustainable development to take place. For example, the IUCN (see p. 10) with generous support of donors in Nordic countries has mounted a programme that aims to achieve sustainable development and conservation in the Sahel region of Africa (Senegal, Mauritania, Mali, Burkina Faso, Niger, Chad, Sudan, Ethiopia, Somalia and Djibouti). Food production is an emotive issue in the Sahel, but nevertheless it does seem possible that yields can be increased on a sustainable basis with better husbandry and management (IUCN 1989). A first major step of the IUCN Sahel Programme was to provide background information on the processes which have led to famine and land degradation. The factors most important in assembling background information have been climate, population, food production, forestry, fuelwood use and status of protected areas. It may seem surprising to have protected areas in this region, but protected areas can make a major contribution to development by way of the following (see also p. 44).

1. Protected areas provide a gene source for plant and animal breeding, especially locally adapted plants and animals.
2. Protected areas can be used as a control so that the effects of new management practices elsewhere can be monitored against conditions in the protected areas.
3. Protected areas can provide clean water and also act as buffers against the effects of floods and droughts.
4. Protected areas can provide sustainable resources such as firewood.

Aid of many kinds has been directed at the peoples of the Sahel and who could not but fail to respond to the recent, tragic situation where so many people were dying. As well as food aid, serious thought is now being given to what is called debt for nature swaps (see p. 90) in an effort to try and relieve the tremendous financial burden of these countries and at the same time establish a sustainable use of land within protected areas. Europe should be playing a greater and more effective role in such developments.

Modern, intensive agricultural practices in the temperate regions have not been without their impact on wildlife, and a number of organizations have attempted to tackle some of these problems. In Britain, for example, the Nature Conservancy Council (NCC 1977) and the Farming and Wildlife Advisory Group (FWAG) have been active in reconciling the needs of modern agriculture with conservation of nature and landscapes. FWAG is essentially a voluntary organization but has full-time staff who visit farms and offer advice about conservation.

Some exciting developments have recently emerged in Britain from the Game Conservancy Trust's Cereals and Game Birds Research Project. This began in 1984 with the specific research objective of devising practical management plans for farmers so that they could continue farming in a relatively intensive manner but with minimum damage to wildlife. The Project's initial concern was for the status of the English partridge (*Perdix perdix*) and to halt its decline which, on farms, had been caused by lack of food for the chicks. The chicks feed on insects and, over many years, extensive use of agrochemicals had caused a decline in what was previously a rich insect fauna. The Project has devised a management system monitoring 'conservation headlands', that is strips about 6 m in width between the crops and the field boundary or hedge (fig 4.7). Insects and other wildlife have increased in the headlands as a result of both the limited use of agrochemicals in the 'conservation headland' and management of hedge and headlands. Increased insect abundance has been of considerable benefit to partridge populations which have started to recover.

As well as providing richer sources of food for game birds, these conservation headlands support a rich variety of other wildlife. In particular the recovery of butterfly populations has been nothing more than dramatic (Dover *et al.* 1990). Other organisms which benefit from the unsprayed headlands are various predatory spiders, wasps and beetles which attack agricultural pests such as aphids (Park 1988). However most fields are very large and predators of aphids may find it difficult to disperse from the conservation headlands to the inner regions of a cereal field. For this reason, recent research (at the University of Southampton) is investigating the effects of creating strips of grass (corridors, see pp. 49, 77) within cereal fields so that predators of aphids can be encouraged to disperse towards the central parts of the fields.

Hedges in an agricultural landscape are more than just habitats for a rich variety of wildlife. They have been used for centuries as a fundamental part of agriculture and, as well as some having great historical interest, hedges are linear habitats and seem to help some groups of animals,

HEDGE

Trim hedges every other year and keep to a maximum height of 2 m. Do not allow hedge to overgrow adjacent grassy strip which is the vital area for nesting.

CONSERVATION HEADLANDS

The area between the crop edge and the first tramline (usually 6 m wide according to boom width). This is an area of crop treated with selective pesticides (see guidelines) to control grass weeds, cleavers and diseases whilst allowing most broad-leaved weeds and beneficial insects to survive. Ploughing of headlands is recommended especially on heavy soils or where grass weeds are a problem. Avoid turning furrow onto grassy strip as this area can create ideal conditions for annual weeds. Choose headlands next to good nesting cover. Avoid headlands infested with difficult weeds (especially barren brome and cleavers).

SPRAYED CROP

Treat as normal. Avoid drift into headland. Use only safer aphicides.

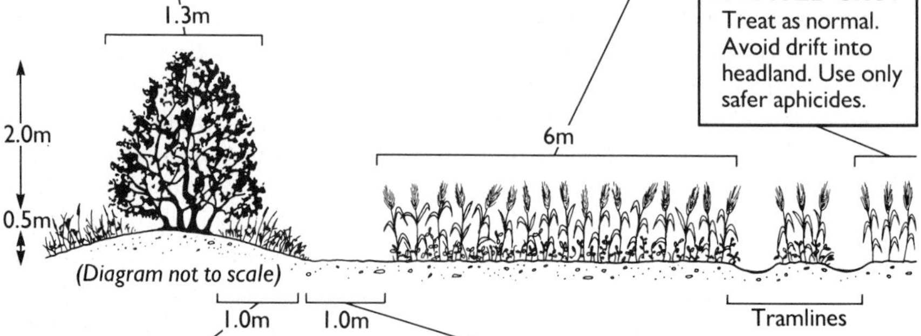

1.3m

2.0m

0.5m

6m

(Diagram not to scale)

1.0m 1.0m

Tramlines

GRASSY BANK/NESTING STRIP

The area used for nest sites by gamebirds and for overwintering by beneficial insects. At least 1 m wide and preferably sited on a bank. Should be composed of perennial grasses and other non-weedy herbaceous species. Avoid spray and fertiliser drift into this area. Allow build up of dead grass material essential for successful nesting, but top the vegetation every 2–3 years to avoid scrub encroachment.

BOUNDARY OR STERILE STRIP

Purpose is to prevent invasion of crop by cleavers and barren brome where they have become abundant. Should be at least 1 m wide. Maintain by rotovation or herbicides (e.g. atrazine) in February/early March. Do not spray out grassy bank. Drill crop further out into the field to leave area of bar cultivated ground for the sterile strip. Avoid spray drift by shielding nozzle down to ground level. Not essential for conservation purposes, purely intended for weed management.

MACHINERY

A specially designed sprayer is now available which can selectively spray a six-metre strip along the headland while treating the main crop with standard chemicals. Each part of the machinery is independent of the other, thus saving the need for a separate run along the Conservation Headland.

While spraying sterile strips it is vital to prevent drift into crop and hedge bottom.

A very useful device, which applies the chemical safely and accurately from the tractor, has been designed for this purpose.

For further information on these two pieces of equipment contact the Conservation Headlands Field Officer.

Fig 4.7 An ideal field margin for game and for conservation of wildlife (from the 1989 Game Conservancy Review, with kind permission of Dr Nigel Boatman).

especially butterflies, to move between fragmented habitats or remnants of woodlands, heathlands and unimproved grassland. In other words, hedges can act as corridors for the dispersal of wildlife (see p. 77). Vast areas of featureless landscape are now commonplace and were once seen to be the most effective basis for agriculture. In the future, and as the benefits of conservation become better known, we may well start to see a return to a more complex landscape with a mosaic of small fields, hedges and copses.

4.11 Biological restoration and creative conservation

The natural environment has suffered considerable damage and loss as a result of human exploitation of nature. Biological communities have been polluted, disturbed, degraded and, in many cases, completely destroyed by industrial wastes. When the cause of the damage has stopped or has been removed, nature will, in time, colonize damaged habitats or derelict land. Sometimes the most appropriate form of biological restoration is to let nature take its own course and, indeed, the flora and fauna of naturally colonized sites can be very interesting and can tell us much about ecological processes such as competition and succession. In many cases, however, management in some form is desirable. Development and application of biological restoration methods, which range from erosion in upland and mountainous areas to revegetation of industrial waste sites, have become a very important component of conservation. These require the skills of many people including ecologists, landscape architects and environmental scientists. The restoration of devastated land is a positive side to conservation and can be thought of as conservation gain. Another aspect of conservation gain is creative conservation, that is the establishment of artificial habitats such as reefs (box 4.9).

Although biological restoration and creative conservation do present exciting possibilities, there is one sad fact which is that it is not possible to return a damaged ecosytsem to its original condition. Some restoration can be achieved, but the complexities of ecosystems and species extinctions make it impossible to replace exactly what has been lost. Natural forests (as apart from plantation forests), whether they be rainforests of the Amazon, cloud forests of Costa Rica or dry temperate eucalyptus forests of Australia, cannot be recreated once they have been cleared. Even the less complex ecosystems cannot be recreated, all we can ever hope to do is restore some of the species and some aspects of the ecosystem.

Restoration

While some forms of restoration require extensive ecological research, other forms of restoration can be achieved largely by managing people. For example, as countryside leisure pursuits become increasingly popular, restoration of land damaged by visitors, vehicles and horses is becoming an increasingly common and costly problem. These recreational pressures result in damage to vegetation by trampling, soil loss and erosion, and pollution from litter, waste and vehicle emissions. Unfortunately, it is often the habitats most sensitive to trampling (including dunes, heathlands, uplands and mountainous areas) which are under greatest pressure. The solution can only be partly ecological and would seem also to require management of people. In the future, will we be prepared to pay to use some of these areas? Will there need to be a leisure tax to fund the management and restoration work?

In a review of the restoration of areas damaged by recreational activities, especially national parks, Goldsmith (1983) suggested some useful guidelines for the future, including the following:

1. use local indigenous material, especially if the area is of ecological importance;
2. use small-scale machinery to minimize any further damage during restoration;
3. ensure that non-natural features blend with the natural features;
4. invest in good environmental interpretation and information for the visitors;
5. work with rather than against people using the area.

The problems of restoration of land following pipe-laying has been well researched for many kinds of communities, including heathlands which are sensitive to trampling. The laying of pipelines across some areas of conservation interest was undertaken in a recent operation in the south of England where 90 km of pipeline linked oil wells in Poole harbour to a refinery in Southampton Water. Over 90% of the route was agricultural land, but it was necessary to take the pipe through some protected areas. The operators first carried out an Environmental Impact Assessment to determine the route which would cause least damage to important ecological and archaeological sites. In the case of wetland sites, it was felt that the best solution was to feed the pipeline below the wetland. When it came to heathlands, matting was used to minimize damage by machinery and the heather was first cut then turfs were carefully removed and stored until the pipe laying was completed. Soil stripping was restricted to the pipe trench only. Replacement turfs, or specially prepared turfs, coupled with seeding the soil along the pipeline route has proved to be successful as a basis for reinstatement of the heather. Subsequent management has ensured that there was no trampling of the reinstated soil and grazing of the young heather.

One particularly common example of restoration is the restoration and revegetation of roadside verges following road construction. Restoration of roadside verges, especially through cuttings, has to take into consideration soil and rock types and drainage patterns, so as to avoid erosion and landslips. Revegetation of cuttings has long been used as a method of helping to stabilize the soil and, for that reason, the choice of plant species, usually a mixture of grasses, has been made on the basis of preventing erosion and landslips.

In Britain, topsoil applied to the cuttings and embankments has usually been sown with the Department of Transport's standard grass specifications of 40% ryegrass (*Lolium perenne*), 15% red fescue (*Festuca rubra*), 15% smooth-stalked meadow grass (*Poa pratensis*), 15% crested dog's tail (*Cynosurus cristatus*) and 10% white clover (*Trifolium repens*). That application of topsoil and mix of grasses has resulted in lost opportunities for conservation because the many kilometres of roadside verges are potential nature reserves. It has been demonstrated by some local authorities that grass swards rich in wildflowers can be established without danger of erosion and landslips. In some instances, wildflower seed mixes together with plug plants (small plants germinated and grown in small containers) have been used, but in a few locations natural colonization by wildflowers has been found to occur readily where soil nutrient levels are low (no need to apply topsoil after road building) and if the grass sward is mown once a year.

The basis of successful revegetation of roadside verges rests not only on ensuring suitable soil conditions but also on the selection of plant species and methods of introduction of the plants by seed or other means. This aspect of revegetation has been researched in relation to plant species enrichment of grasslands. That is, the management of large areas of grasslands as arable land, for sport and for amenity purposes has resulted in fertile soil conditions with a plant community dominated by a few species. Some of the methods used for plant species enrichment are described in the exercise found in section A1.3 of the appendix.

The revegetation of roadside verges can serve more than one purpose and can be extended to landscaping as well as restoration of habitats. That is, with appropriate ground management and selection of grass, herb and tree species, the linear habitats of roadside verges can make an important contribution to conservation and landscaping can also improve the visual aspects of roadside verges.

Revegetation of industrial waste sites and derelict or degraded land has to commence with investigations of the conditions which might limit or restrict plant growth. The main factors which have to be considered include physical factors (water, temperature, soil texture), nutrients (either too much or too little) and toxicity (pH, heavy metals, salinity). Identification of these factors cannot be undertaken without systematic investigations, sometimes requiring the establishment of experimental plots where different treatments of the soil are examined. For example, experimental grass plots using the grass species *Festuca rubra* as a test species provided a systematic basis for a study of revegetation of slag from steel blast furnaces. In that investigation, the main problems were leaching of nitrogen and the inability of the plants to take up phosphates because of the high pH of the waste. The problem of nitrogen deficiency can be overcome either by applications of organic materials and manures or by planting leguminous

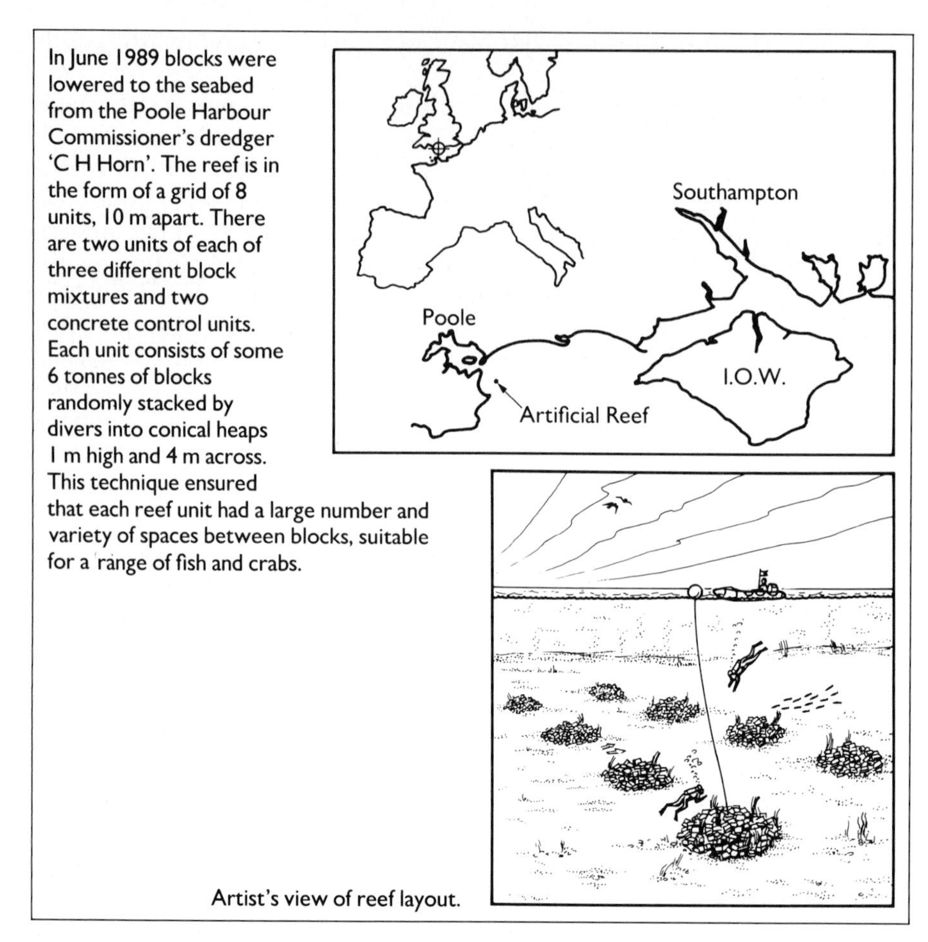

Box 4.9 The Poole Bay (south coast of England) Artificial Reef Project (details reproduced with kind permission of Dr A.C. Jensen, Dr K.J. Collins & Professor A.P.M. Lockwood).

plants (see p. 39). The neutralization of pH on blast furnace slag sites occurs by way of natural leaching and is really the only way of reducing alkalinity unless the slag is covered by soil.

By way of contrast with restoration of pipeline routes, roadside verges, and industrial waste sites, the problems of desertification are very serious and widespread throughout arid regions of the world. **Desertification**, the spread of desert-like conditions as a result of human exploitation, has been tackled by many organizations, including the United Nations Environment Programme. A combination of appropriate irrigation techniques and selection of tolerant plant varieties has enabled some revegetation to take place. In China, for example, tree planting on a huge scale has been carried out to provide fuel, timber and amenity sites and a great belt of trees is to be planted so as to try and stop the advance of the desert.

Fig 4.8 Biosphere II (from Anderson 1989).

Creative conservation

Creative conservation is a term covering many aspects of biological restoration but refers particularly to the colonization of devasted land, the creation of new habitats, the establishment of communities on artificial materials and supplementing resources used by wildlife. For example, construction of ponds, as well as provision of nest platforms, bird boxes and bat boxes can improve the resources available to wildlife.

Creation of artificial reefs has been used in many parts of the world (especially Japan, USA and Britain) to increase catches of fish, crustaceans and molluscs. Pioneering work at the University of New York using coal wastes had minimal success in terms of colonization. Greater success has been achieved in Britain using Pulverised Fuel Ash (PVA) together with gypsum and waste-water sludge from Flue Gas Desulphurization (FGD) plants in electricity generating stations. Colonization of an artificial reef (box 4.9) composed of 50 tonnes of blocks off the south of England has been rapid, initially by shoaling fish such as bib (*Trisopterus luscus*) then by commercial crabs and lobster species. After three months about 80 species of epifauna and flora were well established. The reef blocks are currently being monitored, not only for colonization but also for leaching of heavy metals. These kinds of creative studies are making important contributions to conservation of reef diversity and sustainable use of marine life, not to mention the potential for disposing of products from coal-fired power stations.

Natural ecosystems cannot be replaced, but can they be constructed? Almost like a science fiction story, the construction of a self-contained ecosystem called Biosphere II (fig 4.8) has taken place near Tucson in Arizona (Anderson 1989). This ambitious project is called Biosphere II because Biosphere I is the Earth itself. It is planned that eight people (biospherians) will stay inside Biosphere II for as long as two years where they will grow their own food and live in an artificial wilderness ecosystem made up of about 4000 plant and animal species. What is learnt from

Biosphere II could make a valuable contribution to the better management of Biosphere I.

4.12 Conservation, economics and politics

It is only in the last decade that there has been international recognition of the economic implications of losses in biodiversity. Terms such as 'green economics' are relatively new, and so too are assessments of interactions between economic growth and biodiversity and, hence, conservation. Fortunately there are now many exciting initiatives linking conservation of biodiversity with economics. One central question of these initiatives is how can we value or put a price on nature?

Evaluating nature

Here we are talking about the value of nature in economic terms, that is plain monetary terms and not the moral or aesthetic value of nature (see table 1.1 and section 3.2). Plants, animals, habitats and ecosystems, such as forests, can be valued in monetary terms. For example, fish populations are easily valued in terms of their market value and the same applies to the value of the timber in a forest. A forest could also have an indirect value in terms of its role as a windbreak and a wetlands ecosystem could be valued in terms of its value as a flood barrier, protecting crops and urban areas. For example, it is calculated that the wetlands area of Boston (Massachusetts, USA) are worth $17 million a year for protection against floods. A forest could also have a value put on it in terms of expenditure associated with people using the forest for recreation. In other words, the value of a living ecosystem such as a forest can be thought of in terms of not only marketable value if the trees were removed and sold but also in terms of expenditure associated with the use of that area.

An alternative way of assessing the value of a natural area is to calculate the costs of replacing it if it was destroyed. The replacement costs might take into consideration the costs of growing trees, erosion control, wardens, scientific reports and interest on loans. The next time you are walking through a woodland, across a moor, or on any natural area, give some thought to how much it would cost to replace that woodland or moor.

Sustainable development

The introduction of environmental conservation constraints (not just biological conservation, see fig 1.1) into public investment programmes was just one part of a very refreshing argument put forward in a recent report by Pearce (1989). It was argued that sustainable development entails adjusting economic activity so as to maintain the integrity of populations and ecosystems.

The World Commission on Environment and Development (WCED

1987) defined sustainable development as that which meets the needs of the present without compromising the ability of future generations to meet their own needs. Sustainable use of living organisms and ecosystems is an obvious alternative to exploitation. Human use of living organisms and ecosystems has, in the past, been at such a level that impact had minimal effect. In the industrialized world, levels of exploitation have gone well above the threshold where damage occurs. Sustainable use is a simple idea, meaning, for example, that only a certain proportion of a fish population is taken so that future catches are not affected, or forest timber is used at a rate which does not affect levels of use in the future. In other words, the fish population growth and recruitment is not impaired by the sustainable fishing. We can apply the same idea to agriculture, that is future use of the soil should not be impaired if agriculture is undertaken on a sustainable basis.

Incentives and disincentives

Sustainable use of resources and sustainable development are simple ideas. However, we would be naive in thinking that these ideas would be widely accepted without some incentives for sustainable uses of resources and disincentives for not harming ecosystems or exploiting natural resources. In a very readable book, McNeely (1988) provided examples of incentives (box 4.10) for conserving biodiversity and these included subsidies for reforestation at the community level and debt swaps

Examples of Economic Incentives for Conserving Biological Resources

	Examples		
Type of Incentive	*Community*	*National*	*International*
I *DIRECT INCENTIVES*			
1 In Cash	Subsidies for reforestation	Research grants	World Heritage Fund
2 In Kind	Food for work in a reserve	Forest concessions	WWF equip. for pandas
II *INDIRECT INCENTIVES*			
1 Fiscal Measures	Compensation for damage by wild animals	Price support for intensive agriculture	Commodities agreements; debt swaps
2 Provision of Services	Community development	Conservation education	Technical assistance
3 Social Factors	Enhanced land tenure	Training for staff	Intl. data bases

Box 4.10 Examples of economic incentives for conserving biological resources (from McNeely 1988).

at the international level. Disincentives include taxes ('green taxes'), fines and penalties as well as public and peer pressure. Economic incentives for the promotion of conserving biological diversity can apply at different levels, that is at the community level, national level and the international level.

At the international level, debt swaps for conservation are examples of incentives for conserving biological diversity. Swapping debts for nature involves a conservation organization buying a country's debt at a discount and this is then sold back to the government in local currency with the proceeds going to projects such as establishment of nature reserves. For example, Ecuador has significant debts and has some of the most extraordinary levels of biodiversity (McNeely 1988). There the *Fundacion Natura* has been formed so as to use the debt crisis as an opportunity to attract funds which in turn are invested in conservation.

The ancient island of Madagascar is currently involved in arrangements for 'debt for nature swaps'. Madagascar has lost nearly 80% of its forests, along with a vast array of endemic plant and animal species, many new to science and not described. Madagascar has incurred huge international debts, but there now seems to be a real possibility that conservation organizations, such as the World Wide Fund for Nature, may be able to help both the economy and nature in Madagascar.

The political will

Collaborative investments in huge international projects involving ecosystem modification have brought huge benefits to many parts of the developing world, but some projects have brought about unforseen long-term damage to ecosystems and loss of biodiversity. For example, the Aswan High Dam on the Nile (built during 1960–70) has resulted in depleted silt deposits (natural source of nutrients), and this in turn has caused a decline in fish populations. The Nile Delta has retreated as a result of diminishing natural building materials brought down by the river and the productivity of the delta lakes has declined. These events, and many others like them, demonstrate very clearly the need for detailed environmental assessments and monitoring, especially on a long-term basis.

There are indications that some international agencies are beginning to recognize the importance and long-term advantages of adopting alternative strategies leading to minimal damage to ecosystems and biodiversity. For example the World Bank in 1986 published *Wildlands: their protection and management in economic development*, and in that document said that they would not finance projects that convert lands of special concern, including national parks, biological reserves as well as areas such as watersheds.

One of the important documents which has motivated international and national action was the World Conservation Strategy (see p. 16). The second World Conservation Strategy is currently being prepared, and we may well see many more nations responding in a positive way to the new document and preparing national conservation strategies, an activity which brings together new potentials for economic development and conservation.

However, economics and ecology do not go easily together and one meeting of ecologists and economists held in 1984 was far from a success because the economists rejected the idea that natural resources can be finite. We cannot escape the fact that biological conservation takes a back seat in times of economic stress. There has been an increase in poverty in many regions of the world and at the same time there is a growing financial crisis. In the 1980s and 1990s we have been witness to some of the most horrific examples of environmental degradation and famine, all too often coupled with wars and natural disasters. The most recent of these was the largest oil spill ever during the war in the Gulf. During these troubled times, biological conservation and its potential long-term advantages comes low in the list of priorities in favour of immediate concern for human safety and welfare. Can we ever dare to think that in times of environmental disasters and human tragedies, international economics and politics will attend to immediate human needs but also appreciate the importance of biological conservation and so invest in sustainable use of natural resources?

4.13 Biological conservation and the future

Biological diversity is seriously threatened by modern human activity, but we have seen that many efforts are being made to try to limit this threat. These efforts have not always been wholly successful, but it is encouraging to note that concern is growing and that the problems are becoming more clearly defined. So what of the future? Well, we don't have a crystal ball but we can make some educated guesses and identify some potential solutions and trouble spots.

The future for wildlife cannot be secure while the human activities that have been responsible for the decline in diversity remain unchecked. Population continues to grow steeply in developing countries and demand for resources is unrelenting. Consequently, wildlife is being squeezed into a smaller and smaller space. It may be that in the long term many species could be confined to national parks and wilderness areas; like a sort of global botano-zoo, with a few hardy species such as starlings, rats and rabbits coexisting alongside humans in towns, cities and farms. Studies on species–area relationships have tended to show that smaller areas support fewer species and, consequently, if the global botano-zoo became a reality then further extinctions would be inevitable.

World population, as we have seen, seems set to rise to about 11 billion before stabilizing in about 2150. Of greater significance is that growth will be greatest in areas where diversity is highest. Arresting population growth, however, is a difficult task. The underlying causes are complex, but seem to be related to living standards (see per capita GNP column in table 3.2). The obvious solution would be to redistribute some of the wealth from the richer developed nations to the poorer developing ones, but such charity runs contrary to our innate selfishness. A government that proposed a reduction in personal income to fund overseas development would gain little support, at least in the near future.

It is further predicted that the population will stay at about 11 billion for anything between 200 and 500 years before beginning to fall. The preservation of species ex situ therefore may be a very long-term exercise. This presents the problem of evolutionary stagnation. That is, species taken out of the wild and kept in zoos or stored as germ plasm would no longer be able to evolve alongside their environment. Moreover, characteristics which make them easier to keep, such as docility, may be artificially selected and learned behaviour such as food selection and territoriality would be lost. As a consequence species kept for such a long period of time may be ill-fitted to return to the wild, should it become available again.

As for resources, the present levels of consumption look set to exhaust non-renewable energy and mineral supplies in the near future, but there is no sign that demand will drop. In the long-term this may force us to adopt changes in our lifestyle, but in the short-term there are a number of worrying aspects to the situation. As demand exceeds supply, pressure will mount for the mining of less economic and less accessible stocks; in protected areas perhaps? Already attention has focused on Antarctica, one of the few remaining unspoilt regions of the world.

Present levels of pollution threaten not only wildlife but pose a serious hazard to ourselves. The recent concerns over the ozone layer, global warming, algal blooms, acid rain and radioactivity have certainly raised the profile of this problem. Responses have been slow, however, and we continue to discharge great volumes of harmful substances into the environment. Many pollution issues are now of global concern, but controls are expensive and universal action has been slow. Some countries simply cannot afford it. It would seem that problems such as pollution need to achieve catastrophic proportions before we are able to respond in a united way. It is likely that pollution will get worse before it gets better. We can only hope that we are able to act before the situation is irretrievable.

Overexploitation is seen as a serious threat to biodiversity. The problem here stems from the desire for short-term gains at the expense of sustainable utilization. The reason can be found in our 'selfish' genes. Human behaviour, like the behaviour of all species, is driven by the need to secure enough resources to be able to survive and reproduce. This is normally in competition with others and so the pursuit of resources is heightened. This, perhaps, makes the apparently selfish actions of the ivory poacher and the multinational mining corporations a little more understandable, if not forgivable.

The onus therefore falls on society to make better rules to encourage sustainable utilization, which of course is in the long-term interest. Societies though, are ruled by individuals who may still be driven by their own self-interest. So it would seem that for the sake of biological conservation international rules are needed. This of course is the basis for many conservation initiatives such as CITES (section 4.5) and the IWC (section 4.6). There would seem to be a broad concensus, but countries are free to sidestep agreements and treaties, and countries are ruled by groups and individuals who may still be driven by their own self-interest. This has been seen recently with Japan and whales, and with Zimbabwe and ivory. As the concensus strengthens, however, the majority are able to exert greater pressure on all to conform. The USA have taken an applaudable step by establishing legislation whereby they are duty-bound to cease trading with any nation that breaks a conservation treaty to which it is a party.

You might be left thinking that the future is depressing and rather hopeless. There is certainly no escaping the fact that things are serious and many more species are likely to become extinct. There are, however, two possible rays of hope. Firstly, environmental awareness is gathering momentum and if it were to develop exponentially, like population growth, much could be achieved in a short space of time. Secondly, environmental concerns are bringing the nations of the world closer together. It has often been suggested that many of the human ills would be solved if an extraterrestrial threat appeared. Then the vast sums of money and energy spent on defending national boundaries could be diverted to the common good. It may just be that the current environmental crises have become the equivalent of an 'extraterrestrial threat'. Just imagine how $2.5 billion a day, the amount spent on defence in 1985, could be used for conservation.

There is much we can do as individuals to slow down the loss of biological diversity. Firstly, by lobbying politicians with letters and petitions on matters relating to conservation. It is surprising how much response can be stimulated from this simple act. Secondly, by joining one of the various conservation or environmental organizations. Thirdly, we should keep abreast of current environmental affairs so that we are able to make informed decisions on matters relating to conservation. Simple actions like purchasing species-friendly products can have an effect, especially if you can persuade others to join you.

A quotation by Edmund Burke that appears at the beginning of Norman Myers' *The primary source* is particularly apt here:

> Nobody makes a greater mistake than he who did nothing because he could do only a little.

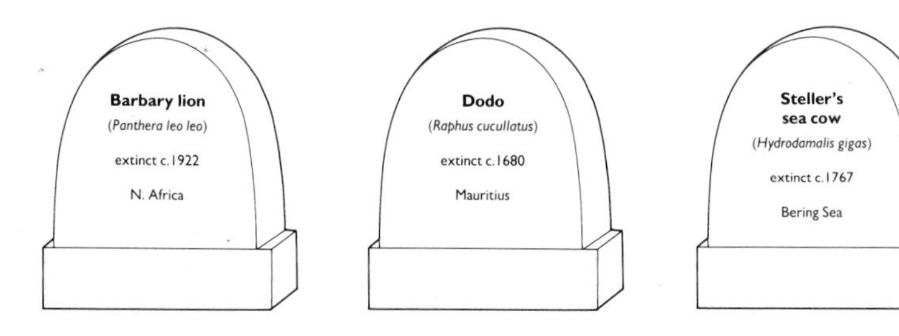

Appendix I

Exercises in ecology and conservation

A1.1 Woodland area and conservation of birds

Although it is tempting to refer to fragments of woodlands or other fragmented terrestrial communities as 'islands', this can be misleading because there is no evidence to suggest that the ecology of real islands is in any way similar to the ecology of fragmented terrestrial communities. Whereas an island community is surrounded by sea and isolated from other land, the remnants of terrestrial communities are surrounded by other communities and in reality there is no strict division between one community and another.

Here, we should concentrate not on potential similarities between the ecology of islands and the ecology of woodlands but on the simple observation that larger woodlands tend to have more species of birds than do small woodlands. In other words if we were to prepare a graph showing the relationship between woodland area and the number of birds in each woodland, we could find that there is a linear relationship between woodland area and the number of bird species. There can, however, be a lot of variation because some small woodlands support more species than might be expected and some large woodlands have fewer species than expected.

Objectives

The objective is to assess the hypothesis that large woodlands are better as nature reserves for birds than smaller woodlands. At the same time we could attempt to answer the question 'What is the optimum woodland area for a nature reserve where the main objective is conservation of birds?'

Table A1.1 *Area of woodland and number of bird species*

The following information has been taken from the BTO records with the kind permission of John Marchant. These records represent many hundreds of man-hours and are part of the Common Bird Census.

Spp = total number of species; Spp.T = number of species holding territories.

(Mean values for various woodlands)

Entry No.	Area ha.	Spp.	Spp.T.	Entry No.	Area ha.	Spp.	Spp.T.	Entry No.	Area ha.	Spp.	Spp.T.
1	1.6	26	18	30	14.2	31	24	59	28.4	32	28
2	4.8	27	19	31	14.4	38	31	60	28.7	44	31
3	5.0	29	15	32	15.3	39	29	61	29.1	33	32
4	5.6	16	14	33	15.2	41	31	62	29.6	39	31
5	6.1	25	20	34	15.4	42	37	63	30.4	42	33
6	6.5	30	25	35	15.4	33	25	64	34.4	57	41
7	6.6	25	19	36	15.6	35	29	65	36.3	34	24
8	6.7	39	29	37	15.8	34	27	66	39.4	43	35
9	8.1	29	28	38	16.1	41	31	67	42.5	48	34
10	8.1	25	21	39	16.2	44	42	68	42.9	50	37
11	8.5	38	31	40	16.6	35	30	69	45	48	39
12	8.5	27	23	41	16.7	34	27	70	45	31	27
13	9.2	29	28	42	17.4	35	30	71	46.7	50	45
14	10	38	27	43	17.4	33	24	72	47	42	31
15	10.1	37	27	44	18	47	36	73	48.8	50	36
16	10	37	27	45	18.2	41	31	74	54	49	32
17	11.1	38	28	46	18.2	43	32	75	67.9	45	39
18	11.1	32	29	47	18.2	50	36	76	68	39	36
19	11.3	30	23	48	18.4	39	35	77	72.9	42	30
20	11.5	36	28	49	20.7	42	33	78	85.8	37	32
21	12.1	36	27	50	21.5	33	23	79	111.3	41	29
22	12.8	35	29	51	21.6	30	24	80	116.6	43	39
23	12.9	28	23	52	22	50	42	81	132	54	40
24	13.4	33	25	53	22	39	32	82	162	47	31
25	13.4	48	39	54	23.7	55	38	83	193	40	39
26	13.5	34	28	55	24	38	32	84	220	40	39
27	13.6	41	37	56	25.2	35	32	85	245	47	41
28	13.8	38	34	57	25.3	36	25				
29	13.8	46	40	58	26.6	38	31				

The data

The data have been extracted from the British Trust for Ornithology (BTO) Common Birds Census and are a simplified version of some far more complex data (table A1.1). We are provided with records of the mean number of bird species (but for simplification not the species' names) observed in woodlands in Britain over a series of years. The number of bird species has been recorded as the total number of species and also the number of breeding species, that is the number holding territories.

Analysis

Simple graphical analysis may be undertaken and it soon becomes obvious that although the general trend is for larger woodlands to support more bird species, there is a lot of variation in the number of bird species found in woodlands of similar area.

Discussion

In view of the variation in data, it is interesting as a first step to consider the reasons for the variation, especially the biological reasons and not just observer bias. No two woodlands of similar area are the same, and obviously the species, age and distribution of trees in the woodland will partly determine the number of bird species. The surrounding land use, the degree of disturbance in the woodland, the type of management and additional habitats such as streams and ponds will also be contributing factors.

We should then consider the hypothesis and attempt to answer the question asked in the aims and objectives. Are there any circumstances where a small woodland would be better than a large woodland for conservation of birds? The data was provided in two forms, breeding birds and total birds; reasons for this should be considered especially with regard to the fact that some birds use woodland other than for breeding. Finally, you might usefully consider woodland management, buffer zones and corridors as part of the nature reserve design.

A1.2 Preparing a management plan: an exercise in ecology and conservation

Management is an integral part of biological conservation, and even a theoretical approach, as opposed to a practical approach, can serve as a useful introduction to the ecological basis of conservation. The establishment of a protected area such as a nature reserve will require a management plan for the area, even if it is just a simple plan to minimize disturbance to the area. Usually, however, the objective is to manage the area so as to gain the most benefits in terms of conservation.

Aims

The main aim of this exercise is to examine an area with a view to preparing a management plan. In the time available, some hypothetical parameters may have to be accepted, such as the precise boundary of the area, the future use of the surrounding land, ownership of the area under consideration and financial limits for the project. The management plan can usefully be done as a group exercise, the group acting as though it were a management team from a conservation organization. At stages during the preparation of the management plan, value judgements may have to be made and these may usefully form the basis of group discussions.

Methods

This can be done as a map exercise, but preferably the group would visit the site at least once. Ideally, there are four stages:

1 the area is defined on a map, general information is provided to the group and a visit to the area is undertaken;
2 the group establishes a conceptual framework for the management plan by addressing a number of questions;
3 data gathering and consultation is undertaken;
4 the management plan is assembled and presented.

What is the objective of management?

Management of natural or seminatural areas could range from simple exclusion of grazing by large herbivores to a combination of conservation, amenity and education facilities. Alternatively, management could be directed at various kinds of habitats or taxonomic groups. Some woodlands, for example, are managed primarily for the butterfly fauna and others managed to create the greatest diversity of habitats to support as much wildlife as possible. The physical, ecological and perceived capacities of the area are important in this respect. The physical capacity refers to the maximum level of use (in space and time) that the area is able to accommodate, and takes into consideration numbers of people, cars, boats and so on. Ecological capacity is reached when various ecological attributes, such as species richness and diversity of habitats, begin to decline as a result of use of the area. Perceived capacity is interesting, and refers to our perceived loss of value of the area as a result of crowding (a well-used woodland, for example, may seem less attractive than a woodland which was used by only a few people). Addressing these questions may require further information about the area and firm statements about the management objective may have to be deferred until such information is obtained.

The management of the area may have to take into consideration any legal constraints that may exist. For example, the local authorities may have applied a tree preservation order on all trees in the area. Alternatively, the local structure plans may have incorporated outline planning permission for a new industrial complex in the area and subsequent pollution may affect the area being considered. There may be public rights of way across the land and other rights of access, such as for shooting or fishing. Management activities will always have financial constraints and therefore a management plan should include some discussion about costs and possibly ways of generating income.

If the area is to have a combined conservation and educational use, some thought might be given to including environmental interpretation in the management plan. Environmental interpretation can range from simple leaflets which describe the more interesting biological features of the area to informative signs being erected in the area.

Data collection

A detailed management plan cannot be prepared without information on the area and obviously sources of information need to be considered. Some information can be collected first hand, but other information could be acquired as a result of consultation with organizations and individuals. There may be databases which could be consulted and clearly there are many skills involved in data acquisition.

It is interesting to discuss the relative merits of historical information and the extent to which new information should be obtained. A basic question is to ask which species occur in the area, but it is, of course, impractical to survey all taxonomic groups. Some groups, such as small mammals, are difficult to record. Other groups, such as lichens and mosses, are difficult to identify. These are practical problems which can limit the extent of a biological inventory and ecological survey.

The 'obvious' and easily recorded taxonomic groups form the basis for any biological inventory. Thus, in the case of a woodland, the tree species would form the basis of data collection. The structure of a woodland community is an important attribute because, in general, greater structural diversity will support a greater species-richness of wildlife. Structure refers to variation in tree ages, variation in species, variation in ground topography, variation in vegetation layers (ground cover, shrub layer and so on) and variation in forms of management such as coppicing. One aspect of woodland structure is variation in the ages of different tree species and age of trees can be indirectly measured by recording tree girth at a standard height (typically about 1 m above ground level or at chest height). Species lists of birds, flowering plants, butterflies and other 'obvious' groups are also important components of the biological inventory.

A list of the habitats and a map showing the distribution of the habitats is essential. The advantages of field data sheets become obvious when collecting data on the types and distribution of habitats: data can be collected quickly and uniformly by several people. One example of a good field data sheet is that devised by Bunce & Shaw (1973) who were interested in biological inventories and ecological surveys (table A1.2). This information could also be used for planning how best to collect additional biological information.

It is as equally impractical to obtain exhaustive ecological information as it is to obtain comprehensive species lists. Field work involving collection of basic data on community ecology, such as species diversity, species richness and biomass can, however, be important for the management plan and

Table A1.2 *From Bunce & Shaw (1973).*

1 Site No.	2 Plot No.	3 Recorder	4 Date
5 Slope ° or		6 Aspect ° Mag.	
A Trees – management			
7 Cop. stool	8 Singled cop.	9 Rec. cut.cop.	10 Stump hard.new
11 Stump hard.old	12 Stump con.new	13 Stump con.old	14
B Trees – regeneration			
15 Alder	16 Ash	17 Aspen	18 Beech
19 Birch	20 Hawthorn	21 Hazel	22 Holly
23 Hornbeam	24 Lime	25 Oak	26 Rowan
27 Rhododendron	28 Sweet chestnut	29 Sycamore	30 Wych elm
31 Other hrwd.	32 Scots pine	33 Yew	34 Other con.
C Trees – dead (= habitats)			
35 Fallen brkn.	36 Fallen uprtd.	37 Log. v. rotten	38 Fall.bnh.>10 cm
39 Hollow tree	40 Rot hole	41 Stump <10 cm	42 Stump >10 cm
D Trees – epiphytes and lianes			
43 Bryo.base	44 Bryo.trunk	45 Bryo.branch	46 Lichen trunk
47 Lichen branch	48 Fern	49 Ivy	50 Macrofungi
E Habitats – rock			
51 Stone <5 cm	52 Rocks 5.50 cm	53 Boulders >50 cm	54 Scree
55 Rock out sp.<5 m	56 Cliff >5 m	57 Rock ledges	58 Bryo.covd.rock
59 Gully	60 Rock piles	61 Exp.grav/sand	62 Exp.min.soil
F Habitats – aquatic			
63 Sml.pool <1 m^2	64 Pond 1–20 m^2	65 Pond/lake >20 m^2	66 Strm/riv. slow
67 Strm/riv.fast	68 Aquatic veg.	69 Spring	70 Marsh/bog
71 Dtch/drain dry	72 Dtch/drain wet	73	74
G Habitats – open			
75 Gld. 5–12 m	76 Gld. >12 m	77 Rky.knoll <12 m	78 Rky.knoll >12 m
79 Path <5 m	80 Ride >5 m	81 Track non. prep	82 Track metalled
H Habitats – human			
83 Wall dry	84 Wall mortared	85 Wall ruined	86 Embankment
87 Soil excav.	88 Quarry/mine	89 Rubbish dom.	90 Rubbish other
I Habitats – vegetation			
91 Blkthorn.thkt.	92 Hawthorn thkt.	93 Rhodo.thkt.	94 Bramble clump
95 Nettle clump	96 Rose clump	97 W.herb clump	98 Umbel.clump
99 Bracken dense	100 Moss bank	101 Fern bank	102 Grass bank
103 Leaf drift	104 Herb veg. >1 m	105 Macfungi.soil	106 Macfungi.wood
J Animals (mainly signs)			
107 Sheep	108 Cattle	109 Horse/pony	110 Pig
111 Red deer	112 Other deer	113 Rabbit	114 Badger
115 Fox	116 Mole	117 Squirrel	118 Anthill
119 Corpse/bones	120 Spent ctrdgs.	121	122

Comments

there are a number of useful books and scientific papers which describe the methods (see the Bibliography).

Presentation of the management plan

Public enquiries or public consultation commonly form an important part of the preparation of a management plan. In essence, details of the plan are made available for inspection and comments are invited. These comments may be incorporated into a modified management plan which is then presented at a meeting. At the meeting there are further opportunities for comments to be made about the management plan.

As part of the exercise, the management plan could be presented by a 'planning committee' or two or more 'planning committees' could present alternative management plans, complete with their costs and benefits. A further group could act as an executive committee and decide on which management plan to adopt.

A1.3 Plant species enrichment of grass swards

The aim is to give a brief account of the factors which affect the plant species composition of grass swards and to encourage better management of the many expanses of manicured, species-poor grass swards belonging to schools, colleges and universities. The example summarised in Table A1.3 shows the interesting results of some different mowing regimes as well as providing basic ideas for a management plan.

Prior to the 1930s, it was generally thought that the plant species composition of a managed grass sward was the product of the seed mixture and little else. Subsequently it has been shown that grazing could also have a rapid and profound effect on species composition. This is because grazing animals are selective and do not graze evenly over the whole sward. The intensity of grazing and the timing of grazing was also found to be important; grazing early in the year would weaken those plants which produced leaves early in the season. Effects of selective grazing are made more complex by the additional effects of trampling and dunging. The selective effects of grazing can be seen when population levels are reduced. For example, when there was an outbreak of myxomatosis and rabbit populations were greatly reduced, it was shown that there was a decrease in plant species-richness but an increase in the number of flowering plants as a result of reduced grazing pressures.

Mowing or cutting does not have the same effect as grazing because mowing is not selective. Nevertheless frequency of cutting and timing of cutting can change the plant species composition because different species have different seasonal growth patterns. The ability of a plant to compete will be diminished if it is cut during the time when growth is most rapid.

The application of fertilizers and any changes in the pH of the soil will also affect the plants species composition and structural complexity of a grass sward. Nutrient poor grassland has many species because such conditions prevent any one species from becoming dominant. For example, some ancient meadows in England may support as many as 145 species of flowering plants and 20 or more species of butterflies. Nutrient enrichment favours a few vigorous species and so grassland which has been treated with fertilizer will become dominated by one or two species.

The long-term effects of adding nutrients to unimproved and plant species-poor grass swards has been researched in the now-classic Park Grass Experiments set out in 1856 at the Rothamsted Experimental Station at Hertfordshire in England. This station, founded in 1843, is the oldest agricultural research station in Britain and it is there that several experiments on the long-term effects of nutrients on crop yields have been investigated. Of all the plots in the Park Grass Experiment, the unmanured plots have the richest flora, lime alone has had little effect and nitrogen gives reasonable yields of various plant species. Perhaps most interesting has been the liming of very acid soils, resulting in a change in plant species composition of the swards. Red clover (*Trifolium pratense*) has become well established, the fescue grasses have increased, cocksfoot (*Dactylis glomerta*) is now common, smooth-stalked meadow grass (*Poa pratensis*) is plentiful and dandelions (*Taraxacum officinale*) are present.

Changes in species composition and species richness of grass swards can be achieved through grazing, cutting and manipulation of nutrients. An alternative approach is to introduce plant species by way of seeds or plants. It would seem simple to increase species richness by distributing seeds or by introducing young plants. Nothing could be further from the truth and the problems involved give a good insight into germination and plant ecology. Firstly, different species have different soil requirements, some favouring acid soils, some neutral and some alkaline. The seeds of different species may have to experience certain conditions before they will germinate, some need to experience a frost, some a severe fire. Different species have different cycles, some germinating early in the year some later in the year. Whether seeds or small plants are used, an interesting factor effecting germination and establishment is the size of the space or gap where the seed or plant is introduced. Small areas of bare ground, no matter how created, provide an opportunity for a seed to germinate and grow, but the size of that gap can affect the success of both the germination and establishment of the plants in the grass sward.

Land taken out of agriculture may take some time before a species-rich grass sward can be developed. This is because chemicals and fertilizers can have long-lasting effects. However, the many areas of close-cropped amenity grasslands and 'manicured lawns' of rye grass and clover offer opportunities for increasing the plant species-richness and contributing to the conservation of wildlife (Wells *et al.* 1981). The way a grassland is managed can be very important not only for the plants but also the animals, ranging from small invertebrates to birds and mammals. Changes in plant species composition and grassland structure have been found to have striking effects on the insect fauna (Duffey 1974), thus increasing the conservation value of the area.

An example of management of grass swards by mowing

In 1981 experimental plots were established at Southampton University to investigate the effects of different mowing regimes on grass swards. It was expected that the combination of different plant phenologies (time of germination, growth and reproduction) and mowing timing and frequency would soon result in changes to the plant species composition. Additional studies were directed at changes in the invertebrate fauna of these plots and other plots with different fertilizer treatments.

The plots are 12 m by 9.5 m (circa 0.01 ha) and are separated by 1 m paths. There are four mowing regimes: mown monthly to a height of 4 cm, mown annually in June to a height of 10 cm, mown annually in August to a height of 10 cm, unmown (control). The plots are located on freely draining sandy soil supporting neutral grassland which was previously used as unimproved grazing land. The effects of the different mowing regimes were beginning to appear after four years (table A1.3); for example, mowing in June has resulted in a sward with the greatest species richness. Such plots provide the basis for excellent nature reserves.

A1.4 Identification of conservation status (threat numbers)

The *British Red Data Book 1, Vascular Plants* (Perring & Farrell 1977) lists plants according to the threats faced by each species (table A1.4). There is a similar volume for Ireland (Curtis & McGough 1988). The *British Red Data Book* was a first attempt to try and quantify the threat or conservation needs of plant species. Threat numbers provide a means of identifying priorities, particularly when funds for implementing conservation measures are limited. That is, when resources for conservation are limited, those plants with the highest threat number receive more attention than species with lower threat numbers.

Aim

From data provided about various plant species, the aim is to assign a threat number to each species; the higher the number the greater the threat and thus the greater the conservation needs. The results can then be compared with the information in the *Red Data Book*.

Methods

Data sheets, in the form shown in box A1.1, can be prepared for a variety of species representing the range of threat numbers in the *Red Data Books*. Not all species need be included in the *Red Data Book*. The

Table A1.3 *Percentage cover of plant species in mown grass swards after four years of different mowing regimes. The presence (but with no measurable cover) is indicated by a tick. From an Environmental Sciences student's project at Southampton University (B.A. Smith, 1985).*

		Monthly mown	Unmown	August-mown	June-mown
Holcus lanatus	Yorkshire fog	22.3	32.4	30.8	43.0
Festuca rubra	Red fescue	17.9	9.1	13.0	13.7
Agrostis spp.	Bents	27.6	8.3	7.6	16.6
Dactylis glomerata	Cocksfoot	3.9	15.0	13.7	7.1
Phleum pratense	Timothy		0.4	0.2	0.1
Lolium perenne	Perennial rye grass	0.8			0.2
Arrhenatherum elatius	False oat grass		5.9	0.3	2.5
Anthoxanthum odoratum	Sweet vernal-grass	10.4	0.4	3.2	3.3
Cynosurus cristatus	Crested dog's-tail	√			0.3
Poa pratensis	Meadow-grass	0.3			0.3
Heracleum sphondylium	Hog weed	0.3	0.6	1.2	0.3
Vicia sativa	Common vetch		0.3	0.1	0.1
Luzula campestris	Field woodrush	0.1	√		1.0
Potentilla reptans	Creeping cinquefoil	√			0.1
Cerastium holosteoides	Common mouse-ear chickweed	0.1	√		0.1
Ranunculus bulbosus	Bulbous buttercup	2.2	0.1	0.1	2.4
Ranunculus repens	Creeping buttercup				
Ranunculus acris	Meadow buttercup		0.4		0.2
Hypochaeris radicata	Cat's ear	0.3	0.5	0.3	0.6
Trifolium pratense	Red clover	0.8	0.4	0.3	1.2
Trifolium repens	White clover		√		0.1
Achillea millefolium	Milfoil	2.8		1.8	√
Centaurea nigra	Hardheads	1.4	4.6	15.0	0.8
Lotus corniculatus	Birdsfoot trefoil	1.3		5.0	0.1
Leontodon autumnalis	Autumnal hawkbit				0.1
Leontodon hispidus	Rough hawkbit				
Taraxacum officinale	Dandelion	0.4			1.0
Malva moschata	Musk mallow		2.8	√	
Senecio jacobaea	Ragwort		√		
Rumex acetosa	Sorrel	0.2	0.6		0.6
Plantago lanceolata	Ribwort plantain	4.2	8.3	1.5	2.5
Holcus lanatus (seedlings)	Yorkshire fog				
Stellaria graminea	Lesser stitchwort	0.1			
Cirsium arvense	Creeping thistle	0.1			
Rubus inermis	Bramble				
Urtica dioica	Stinging nettle				
Rumex obtusifolius	Broad-leaved dock				
Bare ground		0.3	0.3	0.6	1.7
Mosses		1.1			
Litter		1.1	9.6	5.3	
	Total number of species	**23**	**21**	**17**	**27**

Table A1.4 *A table of threat numbers for British Plants (from Perring, F.H. and Farrell, L. 1977).*

Species	*Great Britain (GB)* 1		*Total* 2		*Attractiveness* 3	*Conservation* 4	*Remoteness* 5	*Accessibility* 6	*Threat number* 7
Minuartia stricta	1/1	0	1	4	1	1	1	2	9
Muscari atlanticum	10/17	1	17	0	2	2	2	2	9
Narcissus obvallaris	7/9	0	7	2	2	1	2	2	9
Neotinea maculata	1/1	0	1	4	2	2	0	1	9
Oenothera stricta	10/29	2	12	1	2	1	1	2	9
Ophrys fuciflora	4/6	1	10	1	2	1	2	2	9
Paeonia mascula	1/2	1	1	4	2	0	0	2	9
Phyllodoce caerulea	3/3	0	4	3	2	1	1	2	9
Polygonatum verticillatum	4/10	1	5	3	2	1	1	1	9
Polygonum maritimum	2/11	2	2	4	0	2	0	1	9
Potentilla rupestris	3/3	0	3	3	2	2	1	1	9
Ranunculus ophioglossifolius	2/4	1	2	4	0	1	1	2	9
Rhinanthus serotinus	5/68	2	10	1	1	2	1	2	9
Selinum carvifolia	2/5	1	2	4	0	1	2	1	9
Senecio cambrensis	5/5	0	6	2	1	2	2	2	9
Taraxacum acutum	2/2	0	2	4	0	2	1	2	9
Taraxacum austrinum	1/2	1	2	4	0	1	1	2	9
Taraxacum glaucinum	2/4	1	2	4	0	1	1	2	9
Tetragonolobus maritimus	9/9	0	9	2	1	2	2	2	9
Trichomanes speciosum	8/15	1	8	2	2	2	1	1	9
Trifolium bocconei	2/3	1	5	3	1	1	1	2	9
Valerianella rimosa	9/96	2	10	1	0	2	2	2	9
Veronica verna	1/8	2	8	2	0	1	2	2	9
Woodsia ilvensis	4/12	2	4	3	2	1	0	1	9

Column 1 refers to Great Britain and gives information about past and present distribution while the second entry contributes to the threat number based on the following: 0 = decline of less than 33%; 1 = decline of 33% to 66%; 2 = decline of over 66%.

Column 2 gives the number of extant localities of the species known to the Biological Records Centre (in effect the number of 1 km^2 in which it has been recorded) and the second entry contributes to the threat number as follows: 0 = 16 or more localities; 1 = 10–15 or more; 2 = 6–9 localities; 3 = 3–5 localities; 4 = 1–2 localities.

Column 3 is an assessment of the attractiveness of the species (for collectors) and is recorded in the following way: 0 = not attractive; 1 = moderately attractive; 2 = highly attractive.

The conservation index is provided in *column 4* in the following manner: 0 = more than 66% of localities in nature reserves; 1 = between 33% and 66% of localities in nature reserves; 2 = less than 33% of localities in nature reserves; 3 = the same as 2 but is used where sites are subject to exceptional threat.

Columns 5 and 6 are subjective judgements of the relative ease with which the species can be reached by the public: 5 refers to the remoteness of the locality and 6 refers to the ease with which the species can be reached at the locality. In both cases 0 = not easily reached, 1 = moderately easily reached, 2 = easily reached.

Column 7 is the threat number and this is obtained by adding the values in columns 1 to 6. The maximum value that can be obtained is 15.

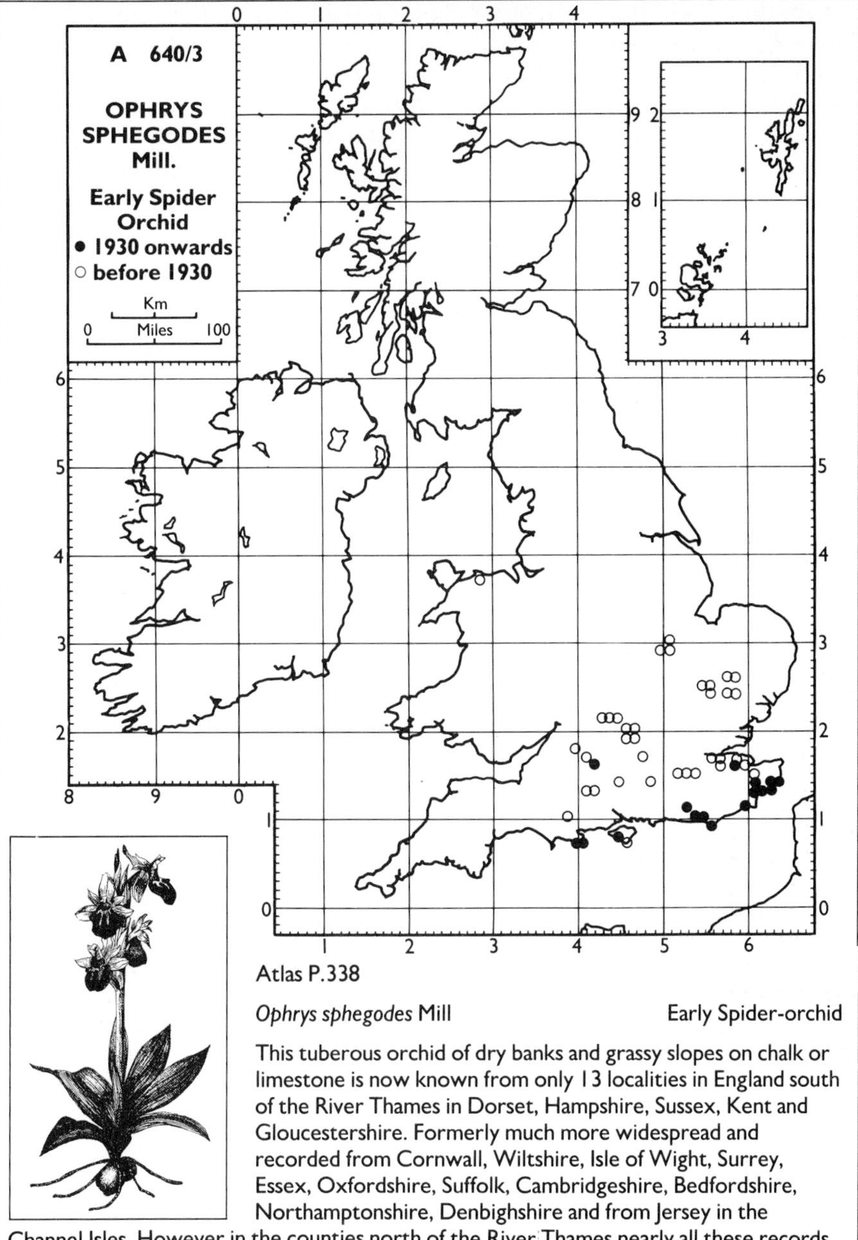

Atlas P.338

Ophrys sphegodes Mill Early Spider-orchid

This tuberous orchid of dry banks and grassy slopes on chalk or limestone is now known from only 13 localities in England south of the River Thames in Dorset, Hampshire, Sussex, Kent and Gloucestershire. Formerly much more widespread and recorded from Cornwall, Wiltshire, Isle of Wight, Surrey, Essex, Oxfordshire, Suffolk, Cambridgeshire, Bedfordshire, Northamptonshire, Denbighshire and from Jersey in the Channel Isles. However in the counties north of the River Thames nearly all these records date from before 1850 and the major decline of this species took place long before the ploughing up of old chalk and limestone grassland.
Nevertheless ploughing and public pressure are now having a deleterious effect, especially on some Dorset populations. Found throughout much of Europe apart from Northern Europe.

81% GB post 1960 1 NNR : 8 SSSI

Box A1.1 A data sheet for the assessment of threat numbers (the map comes from *The Atlas of British Flora*), Perring & Walters 1990).

distribution of the species in box A1.1 is on p.338 of the *Atlas of British Flora* (Perring & Walters 1962). The decline in occurrence of early spider orchid, as recorded by presence/absence in 10 km squares has been 81% in Britain since 1960. This species has some protection and occurs in one National Nature Reserve and in eight Sites of Special Scientific Interest.

The class should be split into small groups (of 10–12 students) to form **committees**. Each committee has the task of establishing a method for awarding a threat number for each of the species. One possible routine (tried successfully many times) is as follows.

1 The committee elects a chairperson and the role of that chairperson is not only to direct proceedings but also to adjudicate when there is a lack of agreement.
2 The committee draws up several criteria (between five and eight) which will be used to calculate a threat number (table A1.5). These criteria might include rate of decline, attractiveness, reproductive potential, importance in relation to other organisms in a community and degree of protection.
3 For each criterion, the committee needs to decide how best to award a score (and use a weighting system if necessary) and the example in table A1.5 is a simple method, bearing in mind the higher the score the greater the threat.
4 The scores for each criterion are summed and, for comparison with threat numbers in the *British Red Data Books*, the final score should be converted to a value out of 15.

Analysis and discussion

Following a verbal presentation by each committee, the threat numbers can be compared with those in the *Red Data Book*. It is then interesting to discuss both the concept and usefulness of threat numbers, as well as the ecological basis of threat numbers. It is also useful to consider the practical applications and limitations of threat number for use with other taxa.

A1.5 Land evaluation for conservation

In section 4.2 we commented on the fact that there are many kinds of formally designated protected areas as well as varied land uses which provide safe havens for many species. Very large protected areas are rare, and in many parts of the world the conservation of habitats is achieved by nature reserves. Where nature reserves are scattered and surrounded by varied land uses, some groups of animals and plants become isolated in them. Where there is a patchwork of conservation areas there is less isolation, some areas being linked by wildlife corridors such as road verges,

Table A1.5 *Suggested criteria for the calculation of a threat number in a practical exercise (from Spellerberg 1981).*

Criteria	*Method of calculation*
Rarity	An index of rarity can be obtained from the information provided in an atlas of distribution. Recorded in less than 10 10 km^2 score 5 between 11 and 50 10 km^2 score 4 between 51 and 100 10 km^2 score 3 between 101 and 400 10 km^2 score 2 recorded in more than 400 10 km^2 score 1
Decline	An index of decline can be obtained from information provided in some atlas of distribution. For an 80 per cent decline score 5 appropriate scores follow as above
Dispersal and recruitment	An index of 1 to 5 could again be used and a high score awarded to those species which on information provided seem to have poor powers of dispersal or a low recruitment
Protection	An index of 1 to 5 is used to indicate the degree of protection afforded by the number of protected localities. If the species occurs on no protected sites then it would score 5

hedges, rivers and canals. The aim of this exercise is to identify areas of high conservation value and to design appropriate methods of management.

Stages of the exercise

This exercise could be based entirely on maps and aerial photographs, but there is no substitute for gathering first-hand information. A useful first stage would be to establish a list of communities or to agree on what constitutes a community. Broad categories such as the following mixture of natural and modified communities could be adopted: urban gardens, cemeteries, streams, rough grassland, road verges, scrub, parkland, woodland, plantations, orchard, allotments.

The second stage of this exercise would be a survey (urban area, part of the countryside or even the grounds of a school). As well as documenting the communities, species lists of some taxonomic groups (for example trees, herbs and grasses, birds, butterflies, lichens) would provide additional information for the evaluation.

The third stage is an assessment of the conservation value of the communities and habitats. A fourth stage could be devoted to the design of management methods for those areas of greatest importance and perhaps those in need of any special management or restoration. Wildlife corridors, such as hedgerows and other linear features, linking habitats could also be assessed in terms of their conservation importance.

Methods of evaluation

Criteria for assessing the conservation value of an area are many but the more commonly used criteria are as follows:

1 presence of protected or rare species;
2 species richness (more species the better);
3 complexity and structural diversity of the community (more variety the better).

Any of these criteria could be used to identify areas of conservation interest, but we can take this a step further and score the relative conservation or ecological value of various areas. For example, one simple but effective evaluation method was that developed by Tubbs & Blackwood in 1971 (table A1.6). Their technique consisted of subdividing an area (basically a map exercise) into 'ecological zones' to each of which is assigned a value from I to V (I being the highest in terms of its value for conservation). For example, areas of unsown vegetation or natural communities would be allocated a relative value of category I. The relative value of agricultural land is scored on the abundance of six features. For example if there were many hedgerows then 3 points would contribute to the relative value. A score of 0 would be added if there were no ponds. The maximum score for agricultural land is 18 (six features times maximum score of three for each feature) and this is equivalent to a relative value of II. The final product of this evaluation method could be a relative ecological evaluation map.

The technique suggested by Tubbs & Blackwood is easily modified so that a more detailed evaluation of either urban or countryside areas can be undertaken. For example, scores for natural or seminatural habitats (woodland, grassland, scrub, riparian) could range from 6 to 10, depending on the extent of disturbance, whereas modified or manmade habitats (parks, gardens, allotments, golf courses, cemeteries, quarries) could be scored from 1 to 5 on the basis of the diversity of features in a modified habitat. Basically, the more natural and the more diverse the greater the value. Although there is no basic ecological reason why large areas should be more valuable than small areas, it is desirable to reduce further fragmentation of natural areas. Therefore, a weighting procedure could be included so that large areas are identified as being more valuable.

For urban areas there are a number of interesting wildlife and conservation evaluation schemes. For example, in Britain the Arboricultural Association has produced a method of assessing the amenity value of woodlands, a method which has been endorsed by the Tree Council. The objectives of the assessment are to give planners and land managers a basis for including amenity values in their calculations (box A1.2).

In Dusseldorf, Wittig (1983) devised a quick method for assessing the importance of open areas based on four categories: the period of time that it would be necessary for the community to develop to its present state, the

Table A1.6 *Ecological evaluation of land. The scoring system suggested by Tubbs & Blackwood (1971)*, Biological Conservation, **3**, *169–72*.

Ecological zone type	*Relative value (I, highest value)*
Unsown vegetation (including non-plantation woodland)	I or II depending on a subjective estimate of the rarity of the habitat and presence of features of scientific importance.
Plantation woodland	II or III, depending on a subjective evaluation of the value as a wildlife reservoir.
Agricultural land	II–V: with a subjective assessment on the extent of habitat diversity assessed on a four point scale (0–3) for six features (permanent grassland, hedgerows, boundary banks, orchards, ponds, fragments of unsown vegetation).

The equivalent relative values for scores derived from agricultural land are as follows: 15–18 (II), 11–14 (III), 6–10 (IV), 0–5 (V).

Evaluation of Woodlands – The Method

Six standard factors are identified in each woodland area, plus any special factors such as historical association, accessibility, or the screening of unwanted views. For each of these factors the woodland is given a score of up to 4 points, and the scores for all the factors are then multiplied together to give an assessment of the amenity value of the woodland.

Factor	Points			
	1	2	3	4
1. Size of woodland	small	medium	large	very large
2. Position in landscape	secluded	average	prominent	very prominent
3. Viewing population	few	average	many	very many
4. Presence of other trees and woodland	area more than 20% wooded	area 5–20% wooded	area 1–5% wooded	area less than 1% wooded
5. Composition and structure of the woodland	young plantation or blatantly derelict woodland	mixed even-aged pole-stage crops	semi-mature or uneven-aged woodland with fairly large trees	mature or uneven-aged woodland with very large trees
6. Compatibility in the landscape	just acceptable	acceptable	good	excellent
7. Special factors	none	one	two	three

Explanatory Notes

1. a "small" woodland is between 0.25 and 1 hectare.
a "medium" woodland is between 1 and 5 hectares.
a "large" woodland is between 5 and 20 hectares.
a "very large" woodland is between 20 and 100 hectares.

2. A "secluded" woodland is one which is visible from a restricted area of not more than about 1 square kilometre.

An "average" woodland will be visible, but not particularly prominent, over an area of 1 to 4 square kilometres.

A "prominent" woodland will be **readily** visible over an area of at least 2 square kilometres; and a "very prominent" woodland over an area of more than 4 square kilometres.

3. Calculations of "viewing population" are unlikely to be exact. A sensible procedure may be to take 2% of the resident population within sight of the woodland; plus 1 person per vehicle on roads, during normal traffic conditions; plus the total numbers of people on foot. Thus, a woodland on the edge of a town, within sight of about 300 houses, containing about 1 000 people; visible from about 2 km of motorway; and from several footpaths and play areas may have a "viewing population" of 20 + 50 + 30 = 100.

The following figures are suggested for the various categories:

"few" = 0–2 viewing population
"average" = 2–20 viewing population
"many" = 20–100 viewing population
"very many" = 100+ viewing population

4. Special factors.
These will include easily accessible woods with public rights of way or open access; well-known landscape features; woods which help to screen unsightly views; and woods with notable displays of wild flowers.

Box A1.2 A method of assessing the amenity value of woodlands widely used in Britain. This method was published in 1967 by the Arboricultural Association and was endorsed by the Tree Council in 1974.

area, the rarity of the open space, and the function of the open space. For period of development, a high value would be given to an area which would require a long time to establish in another location. The more uncommon an area, the higher the score, and this was based on relative abundance of types of open areas for a particular urban area. The function was scored on the basis of least impact from recreation and pollution giving a higher score.

Analysis

Following agreement on the types of habitats and the scoring method, it is then a simple task of recording the information either manually on previously prepared maps or in a more sophisticated manner by way of computers using geographical information systems (GIS). Recent advances in computer technology have made available very useful computers that store information about objects and where they are in relation to one another on the Earth's surface. Handling information in this way enables us to assess the effects of changes in land use and IT CERES is a potential source of information about data handling, information technology and computer databases (see appendix 2).

No matter what kind of method is used for analysis, the main objective is to identify the nature, location and extent (if any) of the most important habitats. A second objective would be to identify (if any) wildlife corridors linking the more important areas.

Applications

Conservation and land-use audits not only serve to draw our attention to important and valuable wildlife areas, but such audits are necessary and integral elements of planning. Nature conservation is one important and legitimate land use and therefore, when planning developments or changes in land use, the planner needs information which will help to prevent damage to or loss of conservation areas.

Appendix 2

A list of organizations relevant to biological and nature conservation

African NGOs Environment Network,
PO Box 53844,
Nairobi, Kenya.

African Wildlife Foundation,
1717 Massachusetts Avenue NW,
Washington, DC 20036, USA

Asian Ecological Society,
c/o Jun-Yi Lin,
Tunghai University,
PO Box 843,
Taichung 40704, Taiwan

Asociacion AMETRA 2001,
(Aplicacion de Medicina Tradicional),
Casilla 42,
Puerto Maldonado,
Matres de Dios, Peru

Bat Conservation International,
PO Box 162603,
Austin,
Texas, 78716, USA

Beckman Foundation for the Environment,
Hillview House,
New Street,
Charfield,
Wootton-under-edge,
Gloucestershire GL12 8ES, UK

Botanical Society of the British Isles,
c/o Department of Botany,
Natural History Museum,
Cromwell Road,
London SW7 5BD, UK

British Association for Nature Conservationists (BANC),
Rectory Farm,
Stanton St John,
Oxford OX9 1HF, UK

British Ecological Society,
Burlington House,
Piccadilly,
London W1V 0LQ, UK

British Trust for Conservation Volunteers,
36 St Mary's Street,
Wallingford,
Oxon OX10 0EU, UK

British Trust for Ornithology,
The Nunnery,
Nunnery Place, Thetford,
Norfolk IP24 2BR, UK

Centre for Our Common Future,
Palais Wilson,
52 rue des Paquis,
CH-1201,
Geneva, Switzerland

Centre for Environmental Education,
1725 DeSales St NW,
Suite 500,
Washington DC 20036, USA

CITES,
Convention on International Trade in Endangered Species,
6 rue Maupas,
Case Postale 78,
CH-1000,
Lausanne 9, Switzerland

Civic Trust,
17 Carlton House Terrace,
London SW1Y 5AW, UK

Council for Environmental Education (CEE),
School of Education,
University of Reading,
London Road,
Reading RG1 5AQ, UK

Countryside Commission,
John Dower House,
Crescent Place,
Cheltenham,
Gloucestershire GL50 3RA, UK

Countryside Commission for Scotland,
Battleby,
Redgorton,
Perth PH1 3EW, UK

Earthwatch Expeditions Inc.,
680 Mt Auburn Street,
PO Box 403,
Watertown,
Massachusetts, 02272, USA

East African Wildlife Society,
PO Box 20110,
Nairobi, Kenya

Ecological Society of America,
Department of Biology,
Notre Dame University,
Notre Dame,
Indiana 46556, USA

Environmental Protection Agency,
401 M Street SW,
Washington DC 20460, USA

The Environment Council,
80 York Way,
London N1 9AG, UK

Fauna and Flora Preservation Society (FFPS),
79–83 North Street,
Brighton,
East Sussex BN1 1ZA, UK

Foundation for Environmental Conservation,
7 Chemin Taverney,
CH-1218 Grand-Saconnex,
Geneva, Switzerland

Friends of the Earth (FoE),
(i) *International secretariat*
26–8 Underwood Street,
London N1 7JQ, UK

(ii) *UK office*
address as for (i)

(iii) *USA office*
530 Seventh Street SE,
Washington DC 20003, USA

Greenpeace
(i) *International*
Keizersgracht 176,
1016 DW Amsterdam,
The Netherlands.

(ii) *UK*
30–1 Islington Green,
London NW1 8XE, UK

(iii) *USA*
1436 U Street NW,
Washington DC 20009, USA

International Board for Plant Genetic Resources,
IBPGR Headquarters,
Via delle Sette Chiese 142,
00145 Rome, Italy

International Centre for Conservation Education,
Greenfield House,
Guiting Power,
Gloucestershire GL54 5TZ, UK

International Council for Bird Preservation (ICBP),
32 Cambridge Road,
Girton,
Cambridge CB3 0PJ, UK

International Union for the Conservation of Nature and Natural Resources (IUCN),
Avenue du Mont-Blanc,
CH-1196 Gland, Switzerland

International Waterfowl and Wetlands Research Bureau,
Slimbridge,
Gloucestershire GL2 7BX, UK

International Youth Federation for Environmental Studies and Conservation,
Klostermolle,
Klostermollevej 48,
DK-8660,
Skanderborg, Denmark

IT CERES, Centre for Education Research, Development and Training in the Environmental Sciences,
School of Education,
University of Southampton,
Southampton SO9 5NH, UK

Jersey Wildlife Preservation Trust,
Les Augres Manor,
Trinity,
Jersey,
Channel Islands, UK

Joint Nature Conservation Committee,
Monkstone House,
City Road,
Peterborough PE1 1JY, UK

Marwell Preservation Trust Ltd.,
Marwell Zoological Park,
Colden Common,
Winchester,
Hampshire SO21 1JH, UK

National Audubon Society,
950 Third Avenue,
New York,
NY 10022, USA

National Wildlife Federation,
1400 Sixteenth Street,
Washington DC 20036, USA

The Nature Conservancy,
1815 North Lynn St,
Arlington,
Virginia 22209, USA

Natural Areas Association,
320 S Third Street,
Rockford,
Il. 61108, USA

Nature Conservancy Council for England (English Nature)
Northminster House,
Peterborough PE1 1JA, UK
See also Joint Nature Conservation Committee

New York Zoological Society,
The Zoological Park,
New York 10460, USA

Patuxent Wildlife Research Centre,
c/o US Fish & Wildlife Service,
Section of Information Management,
Laurel,
Md. 20708, USA

Royal Society for Nature Conservation (RSNC),
The Green,
Witham Park,
Waterside South,
Lincoln LN5 7JR, UK

Royal Society for the Protection of Birds (RSPB),
The Lodge,
Sandy,
Bedfordshire SG19 2DL, UK

Save the Redwoods League (California),
114 Sansome Street,
Suite 605,
San Francisco,
California 94104, USA

Scottish Wildlife Trust,
25 Johnston Terrace,
Edinburgh EH1 2NH, UK

Sierra Club,
730 Polk Street,
San Francisco,
California 94108, USA

Society for Conservation Biology,
c/o Blackwell Scientific Publications Inc,
Three Cambridge Centre,
Cambridge,
Massachusetts 02142, USA

United Nations Environment
Programme (UNEPS),
PO Box 30552,
Nairobi, Kenya

US Fish & Wildlife Service,
Department of the Interior,
Washington DC 20240, USA

Wildfowl and Wetlands Trust,
Slimbridge,
Gloucestershire GL2 7BT, UK

Wildlife Conservation International,
New York Zoological Society,
(see above)

Wildlife Link,
246 Lavender Hill,
London SW11 1LN, UK

World Conservation Monitoring
Centre,
219c Huntingdon Road,
Cambridge CB3 0DL, UK

World Wide Fund for Nature.
(i) *International*
Avenue du Mont-Blanc,
CH-1196,
Gland, Switzerland

(ii) *USA*
1250 24th Street,
NW, Washington DC 20037, USA

(iii) *UK*
Panda House,
Weyside Park,
Catteshall Lane,
Godalming,
Surrey GU7 1XR, UK

Bibliography and suggested further reading

The following is intended to be an introduction to the literature in the hope that you will pursue biological conservation in more depth. As well as books, there are many reports and journals which offer excellent material on conservation. There are also many videos on conservation which are available on loan or for sale. Interactive videos such as *Ecodisc* (a computer simulation of the ecological effects of land management) are also available, the latter from the Multimedia Corporation (previously the BBC Interactive Television Unit), 109x Regent's Park Road, London NW1. The International Centre for Conservation Education produces a wide range of audio-visual material and IT CERES can provide information about teaching media and information technology (appendix 2).

D. Anderson & R. Grove, *Conservation in Africa People, Policies and Practice* (Cambridge, Cambridge University Press, 1987).

I. Anderson, Biosphere II: a world apart. *New Scientist*, **121** (1989) 34–5.

A.D. Bradshaw, D.A. Goode & E.H.P. Thorp, *Ecology and Design in Landscape* (Oxford, Blackwell Scientific Publications, 1986).

R.G.H. Bunce & M.W. Shaw, A standardized procedure for ecological survey, *Journal of Environmental Management*, **1** (1973) 239–58.

R. Carson, *Silent Spring* (Boston, Houghton Mifflin, 1962).

J. Cherfas, *Zoo 2000 A Look Behind the Bars* (BBC, 1984).

S.H. Cousins, Species size distributions of birds and snails in an urban area. In *Urban Ecology*, ed. by R. Bornkamm, J.A. Lee & M.R.D. Seaward (Oxford, Blackwell Scientific Publications, 1982).

T.G.F. Curtis & H.N. McGough, *The Irish Red Data Book. 1. Vascular Plants* (Dublin, The Stationery Office, 1988).

B. Devall & G. Sessions, *Deep Ecology* (Gibbs Smith, Salt Lake City, 1985).

J. Dover, N. Sotherton & K. Gobbett, Reduced pesticide inputs on cereal field margins: the effect on butterfly abundance. *Ecological Entomology*, **15** (1990) 17–24.

E. Duffey, Lowland grassland and scrub: Management for wildlife. In *Conservation in Practice*, ed. by A. Warren & F. B. Goldsmith, pp. 167–83 (London & New York, John Wiley, 1974).

D. Ehrenfield, *Biological Conservation* (Holt, Rinehart and Winston, 1983).

D. Ehrenfield, Thirty million cheers for diversity, *New Scientist*, 12.6.86, 38–43.

M.J. Emery, *Promoting Nature in Cities and Towns, a Practical Guide* (London, Croom Helm, Routledge, Chapman & Hall, 1986).

M. Fenner & I.F. Spellerberg, Plant species enrichment of ecologically impoverished grassland: a small scale trial. *Field Studies*, **7** (1988) 153–8.

R. Fitter, *Wildlife for Man. How and Why We Should Conserve Our Species* (London, Collins, 1986).

F.B. Goldsmith, Ecological effects of visitors and the restoration of damaged areas. In *Conservation in Perspective*. ed. by A. Warren & F.B. Goldsmith, pp 201–14 (Chichester, John Wiley, 1983).

B. Green, *Countryside Conservation, The Protection and Management of Amenity Ecosystems*. (London, George Allen & Unwin, 1981).

S. Holt, Lets all go whaling, *The Ecologist*, **15**(3), (1985).

M. Horbert, H.P. Blume, H. Elvers & P Sukopp, Ecological contributions to urban planning. In *Urban Ecology*, ed. by R. Bornkamm, J.A. Lee & M.R.D. Seaward (Oxford, Blackwell Scientific Publications, 1982).

ICCE, *Planning for Survival. The World Conservation Strategy*. Text and slides, AVP 077 (Cheltenham, International Centre for Conservation Education, 1984).

IUCN, *World Conservation Strategy* (Gland, Switzerland, IUCN, 1980).

IUCN, *The IUCN Sahel Studies* (IUCN Regional Office for Eastern Africa, 1989).

C. Joyce, Dying to get on the list, *New Scientist*, 30.9.89, 42–7.

L. Kaufman & K. Mallory (eds), *The Last Extinction* (Cambridge, Mass., MIT Press, 1986).

K.J. Kirby, *Woodland Survey Handbook*, Research and Survey in Nature Conservation, No. 11 (Peterborough, NCC, 1988).

K. Lindsay, Trading elephants for ivory, *New Scientist*, 6.11.86, 48–52.

J. Lovelock, *Gaia; A New Look At Life on Earth* (Oxford University Press, Oxford, 1979).

S. Lyster, *International Wildlife Law* (Cambridge, Grotius Publications Ltd, 1985).

J.A. McNeely, *Economics and Biological Diversity: Developing and Using Economic Incentives to Conserve Biological Resources* (Gland, Switzerland, IUCN, 1988).

J.A. McNeely, K.R., Miller, W.V. Reid, R.A. Mittermeier & T.B. Werner, *Conserving the World's Biological Diversity* (Gland, Switzerland, IUCN, 1990).

D.H. Meadows, D.L. Meadows, J. Randers & W.W. Behrens, *Limits to Growth* (Earth Island, London, Potomac Associates Edn., 1972).

A.M. Merenlender, D.S. Woodruff, D.A. Ryder, R. Kock & J. Vahala, Allozyme variation and differentiation in African and Indian rhinoceroses, *Journal of Heredity*, **80**, (1989) 377–82.

W.J. Mitsch & G. Gosselink, *Wetlands* (New York, Van Nostrand Reinhold, 1966).

N.W. Moore & M.D. Hooper, On the number of bird species in British woods. *Biological Conservation*, **8** (1975) 239–50.

B. Moss, Restoration of lakes and lowland rivers. In *Ecology and Design in Landscape*, eds. A.D. Bradshaw, D.A. Goode & E.H.P. Thorp, pp. 399–415, 24th Symposium of the British Ecological Society (Oxford, Blackwell Scientific Publications, 1986).
N. Myers, *The Sinking Ark* (Oxford and New York, Pergamon, 1979).
N. Myers, *The Primary Source: Tropical Forests and Our Future* (New York, W.W. Norton, 1985).
N. Myers, *A Wealth of Wild Species: Storehouse for Human Welfare* (Boulder, Colorado, Westview Press, 1983).

NCC, *Nature Conservation and Agriculture* (London, Nature Conservancy Council, 1977).

J.R. Park, *Environmental Management in Agriculture* (London and New York, Belhaven Press, 1988).
F. Pearce, Kill or cure? Remedies for the rainforest, *New Scientist*, 11.9.89, 40–3.
F.H. Perring & L. Farrell, *British Red Data Books: 1 Vascular Plants* (Nettleham, Lincoln, RSNC, 1983).
F.H. Perring & S.M. Walters, *Atlas of the British Flora* (London, BSBI/Nelson, 1962).
C.M. Peters, A.H. Gentry & R.O. Mendelsohn, Valuation of an Amazonian rainforest, *Nature*, 29.6.89, 655–6.

D.A. Ratcliffe, *A Nature Conservation Review*, 2 vols (Cambridge, Cambridge University Press, 1977).
W.V. Reid & K.R. Miller, *Keeping Options Alive; the Scientific Basis for Conserving Biodiversity* (Washington, World Resources Institute, 1989).

O. Sattaur, Genes on deposit: saving for the future, *New Scientist*, 5.8.89, 41–3.
J.L. Simon & H. Kahn, (1980). *The Resourceful Earth. A Response to Global 2000* (Oxford, Basil Blackwell, 1980).
J. Smartt, *Grain Legumes. Evolution and Genetic Resources* (Cambridge, Cambridge University Press, 1990).
M.E. Soule (ed.), *Conservation Biology. The Science of Scarcity and Diversity* (Sunderland, Massachusetts, Sinauer Associates, 1986).
M. Soule, *Viable Populations for Conservation* (Cambridge, Cambridge University Press, 1988).
I.F. Spellerberg, *Ecological Evaluation for Conservation* (London, Edwards Arnold, 1981).
I.F. Spellerberg, F.B. Goldsmith & M.G. Morris, *The Scientific Management of Temperate Communities for Conservation* (Oxford, Blackwell, 1991).

J. Tait, A. Lane & S. Carr, *Practical Conservation. Site assessment and management planning* (Milton Keynes, The Open University, 1988).
A.S. Thomas, Changes in the vegetation since the advent of myxomatosis. *Journal of Ecology*, **48** (1960) 286–306.
W.L. Thomas (ed.), *Man's Role in Changing the Face of the Earth* (Chicago, University of Chicago Press, 1956).
C.R. Tubbs & J.W. Blackwood, Ecological evaluation of land for planning purposes. *Biological Conservation*, **3** (1971) 169–72.
C. Tudge, Breeding by numbers, *New Scientist*, 1.9.88, 68–71.

WCED, *Our Common Future* (Oxford, Oxford University Press, 1987).
A. Warren & F.B. Goldsmith (eds.), *Conservation in Perspective* (Chichester, Wiley, 1983).

S. Wells. A future for coral reefs, *New Scientist*, 30.10.86, 46–50.
T. Wells, S. Bell & A. Frost, *Creating Attractive Grasslands Using Native Plant Species* (Shrewsbury, Nature Conservancy Council, 1981).
D. Western & M. Pearl (eds), *Conservation for the Twenty-First Century* (New York, Oxford University Press, 1989).
E.O. Wilson (ed.) *Biodiversity* (Washington DC, National Academy Press, 1988).
R. Wittig, A quick method for assessing the importance of open spaces in towns for urban nature conservation. *Biological Conservation*, **26** (1983) 57–64.
WWF & IUCN, *Botanic Gardens Conservation Strategy* (Kew, Botanic Gardens Conservation Secretariat, 1989).

K. Young, *Learning Through Landscapes. Using School Grounds as an Educational Resource* (Winchester, Learning Through Landscapes Trust, 1990).

Publications from organizations

Earthscan Publications include a very wide range of titles most relevant to conservation. Earthscan Publications Ltd. (a subsidiary of the International Institute for Environment and Development) has agents throughout the world and the London Office is at 3 Endsleigh St, London WC1H 0DD.

OECD Publications (Organization for Economic Cooperation and Development) include titles on Renewable Natural Resources and Agriculture and Environmental Policies. Central Office: OECD Publications Service, 2, rue Andre-Pascal, 75775 Pars CEDEX 16, France.

UNESCO has published a keynote series of books entitled *The Man and the Biosphere* series, catalogue available from UNESCO Press, Commercial Services, 7, place de Fontenoy, 75700 Paris, France.

World Resources Institute has a range of publications about global resources and the environment. Catalogues available from World Resources Institute Publications, 1709 New York Avenue, NW Washington, DC 20006, USA.

Journals

Ambio, Royal Swedish Academy of Sciences, Box 50005, S-104-05, Stockholm, Sweden.
The American Biology Teacher, Journal of the Association of Biology Teachers, 11250 Roger Bacon Dr. No. 19, Reston, VA 22090, USA.

BBC Wildlife, BBC Wildlife Subscriptions, P.O. Box 125, Tonbridge, Kent TN9 1YP.
Biological Conservation, Elsevier Applied Sciences, Crown House, Linton Road, Barking, Essex IG11 8JU.
The Biologist, Institute of Biology, 20 Queensberry Place, London SW7 2DS.
BioScience, American Institute of Biological Sciences, 730 11th St., NW Washington DC, 20001-4584.

Conservation Biology, published by the Society for Conservation Biology (see appendix 2).

Earthwatch, published by Earthwatch Expeditions Inc. (see appendix 2).
ECOS, publication of the British Association for Nature Conservationists (see appendix 2).

Environmental Conservation, Elsevier Sequoia, S.A., P.O. Box 564, 1001, Lausanne 1, Switzerland.

Habitat, published by the Environment Council (see appendix 2).

Journal of Biological Education, Institute of Biology (see above).

Natural Areas Journal, Natural Areas Association (see appendix 2).
Nature and Resources, published under the auspices of UNESCO by Parthenon Publishing Group, Casterton Hall, Carnforth, Lancs. LA6 2LA, UK.
Naturopa Newsletter, Council of Europe, Documentation and Information Centre for Environment and Nature, BP, 431R6 67006, Strasbourg, Cedex, France.

Oryx, the Journal of the Fauna and Flora Preservation Society (see appendix 2).

Parks, published by Science & Technology Letters on behalf of the IUCN Commission on National Parks and Protected Areas. In USA: Science Reviews Inc., 707 Foulk Rd., Suite 102, Wilmington, Delaware 19803. In UK: Science & Technology Letters, PO Box 81, Northwood, Middlesex HA6 3DN.

Scientific American, especially Special Issue September 1989 (Vol **261**, No. 3), *Managing Planet Earth*, Scientific American Inc., 415 Madison Avenue, New York, NY 10017 USA.
Species. Newsletter of the IUCN Species Survival Commission, IUCN, Gland.

Index